LORD OF THE FLIES

William Golding

SPARK PUBLISHING

122 Fifth Avenue
New York, NY 10011
www.sparknotes.com

ISBN 978-1-4114-6986-0

Please submit changes or report errors to www.sparknotes.com/errors.

Printed in Canada

14

CONTENTS

CONTEXT

WILLIAM GOLDING WAS BORN on September 19, 1911, in Cornwall, England. Although he tried to write a novel as early as age twelve, his parents urged him to study the natural sciences. Golding followed his parents' wishes until his second year at Oxford, when he changed his focus to English literature. After graduating from Oxford, he worked briefly as a theater actor and director, wrote poetry, and then became a schoolteacher. In 1940, a year after England entered World War II, Golding joined the Royal Navy, where he served in command of a rocket-launcher and participated in the invasion of Normandy.

Golding's experience in World War II had a profound effect on his view of humanity and the evils of which it was capable. After the war, Golding resumed teaching and started to write novels. His first and greatest success came with *Lord of the Flies* (1954), which ultimately became a bestseller in both Britain and the United States after more than twenty publishers rejected it. The novel's sales enabled Golding to retire from teaching and devote himself fully to writing. Golding wrote several more novels, notably *Pincher Martin* (1956), and a play, *The Brass Butterfly* (1958). Although he never matched the popular and critical success he enjoyed with *Lord of the Flies,* he remained a respected and distinguished author for the rest of his life and was awarded the Nobel Prize for Literature in 1983. Golding died in 1993, one of the most acclaimed writers of the second half of the twentieth century.

Lord of the Flies tells the story of a group of English schoolboys marooned on a tropical island after their plane is shot down during a war. Though the novel is fictional, its exploration of the idea of human evil is at least partly based on Golding's experience with the real-life violence and brutality of World War II. Free from the rules and structures of civilization and society, the boys on the island in *Lord of the Flies* descend into savagery. As the boys splinter into factions, some behave peacefully and work together to maintain order and achieve common goals, while others rebel and seek only anarchy and violence. In his portrayal of the small world of the island, Golding paints a broader portrait of the fundamental human struggle between the civilizing instinct—the impulse to obey rules, behave morally, and act lawfully—and the savage instinct—the impulse to seek brute power over others, act selfishly, scorn moral rules, and indulge in violence.

Golding employs a relatively straightforward writing style in *Lord of the Flies,* one that avoids highly poetic language, lengthy description, and philosophical interludes. Much of the novel is allegorical, meaning that the characters and objects in the novel are infused with symbolic significance that conveys the novel's central themes and ideas. In portraying the various ways in which the boys on the island adapt to their new surroundings and react to their new freedom, Golding explores the broad spectrum of ways in which humans respond to stress, change, and tension.

Readers and critics have interpreted *Lord of the Flies* in widely varying ways over the years since its publication. During the 1950s and 1960s, many readings of the novel claimed that *Lord of the Flies* dramatizes the history of civilization. Some believed that the novel explores fundamental religious issues, such as original sin and the nature of good and evil. Others approached *Lord of the Flies* through the theories of the psychoanalyst Sigmund Freud, who taught that the human mind was the site of a constant battle among different impulses—the id (instinctual needs and desires), the ego (the conscious, rational mind), and the superego (the sense of conscience and morality). Still others maintained that Golding wrote the novel as a criticism of the political and social institutions of the West. Ultimately, there is some validity to each of these different readings and interpretations of *Lord of the Flies.* Although Golding's story is confined to the microcosm of a group of boys, it resounds with implications far beyond the bounds of the small island and explores problems and questions universal to the human experience.

PLOT OVERVIEW

I N THE MIDST OF A RAGING WAR, a plane evacuating a group of schoolboys from Britain is shot down over a deserted tropical island. Two of the boys, Ralph and Piggy, discover a conch shell on the beach, and Piggy realizes it could be used as a horn to summon the other boys. Once assembled, the boys set about electing a leader and devising a way to be rescued. They choose Ralph as their leader, and Ralph appoints another boy, Jack, to be in charge of the boys who will hunt food for the entire group.

Ralph, Jack, and another boy, Simon, set off on an expedition to explore the island. When they return, Ralph declares that they must light a signal-fire to attract the attention of passing ships. The boys succeed in igniting some dead wood by focusing sunlight through the lenses of Piggy's eyeglasses. However, the boys pay more attention to playing than to monitoring the fire, and the flames quickly engulf the forest. A large swath of dead wood burns out of control, and one of the youngest boys in the group disappears, presumably having burned to death.

At first, the boys enjoy their life without grown-ups and spend much of their time splashing in the water and playing games. Ralph, however, complains that they should be maintaining the signal fire and building huts for shelter. The hunters fail in their attempt to catch a wild pig, but their leader, Jack, becomes increasingly preoccupied with the act of hunting.

When a ship passes by on the horizon one day, Ralph and Piggy notice, to their horror, that the signal fire—which had been the hunters' responsibility to maintain—has burned out. Furious, Ralph accosts Jack, but the hunter has just returned with his first kill, and all the hunters seem gripped with a strange frenzy, reenacting the chase in a kind of wild dance. Piggy criticizes Jack, who hits Piggy across the face. Ralph blows the conch shell and reprimands the boys in a speech intended to restore order. At the meeting, it quickly becomes clear that some of the boys have started to become afraid. The littlest boys, known as "littluns," have been troubled by nightmares from the beginning, and more and more boys now believe that there is some sort of beast or monster lurking on the island. The older boys try to convince the others at the meeting to think rationally, asking where such a monster could possibly hide during the daytime. One

3

of the littluns suggests that it hides in the sea—a proposition that terrifies the entire group.

Not long after the meeting, some military planes engage in a battle high above the island. The boys, asleep below, do not notice the flashing lights and explosions in the clouds. A parachutist drifts to earth on the signal-fire mountain, dead. Sam and Eric, the twins responsible for watching the fire at night, are asleep and do not see the parachutist land. When the twins wake up, they see the enormous silhouette of his parachute and hear the strange flapping noises it makes. Thinking the island beast is at hand, they rush back to the camp in terror and report that the beast has attacked them.

The boys organize a hunting expedition to search for the monster. Jack and Ralph, who are increasingly at odds, travel up the mountain. They see the silhouette of the parachute from a distance and think that it looks like a huge, deformed ape. The group holds a meeting at which Jack and Ralph tell the others of the sighting. Jack says that Ralph is a coward and that he should be removed from office, but the other boys refuse to vote Ralph out of power. Jack angrily runs away down the beach, calling all the hunters to join him. Ralph rallies the remaining boys to build a new signal fire, this time on the beach rather than on the mountain. They obey, but before they have finished the task, most of them have slipped away to join Jack.

Jack declares himself the leader of the new tribe of hunters and organizes a hunt and a violent, ritual slaughter of a sow to solemnize the occasion. The hunters then decapitate the sow and place its head on a sharpened stake in the jungle as an offering to the beast. Later, encountering the bloody, fly-covered head, Simon has a terrible vision, during which it seems to him that the head is speaking. The voice, which he imagines as belonging to the Lord of the Flies, says that Simon will never escape him, for he exists within all men. Simon faints. When he wakes up, he goes to the mountain, where he sees the dead parachutist. Understanding then that the beast does not exist externally but rather within each individual boy, Simon travels to the beach to tell the others what he has seen. But the others are in the midst of a chaotic revelry—even Ralph and Piggy have joined Jack's feast—and when they see Simon's shadowy figure emerge from the jungle, they fall upon him and kill him with their bare hands and teeth.

The following morning, Ralph and Piggy discuss what they have done. Jack's hunters attack them and their few followers and steal

Piggy's glasses in the process. Ralph's group travels to Jack's stronghold in an attempt to make Jack see reason, but Jack orders Sam and Eric tied up and fights with Ralph. In the ensuing battle, one boy, Roger, rolls a boulder down the mountain, killing Piggy and shattering the conch shell. Ralph barely manages to escape a torrent of spears.

Ralph hides for the rest of the night and the following day, while the others hunt him like an animal. Jack has the other boys ignite the forest in order to smoke Ralph out of his hiding place. Ralph stays in the forest, where he discovers and destroys the sow's head, but eventually, he is forced out onto the beach, where he knows the other boys will soon arrive to kill him. Ralph collapses in exhaustion, but when he looks up, he sees a British naval officer standing over him. The officer's ship noticed the fire raging in the jungle. The other boys reach the beach and stop in their tracks at the sight of the officer. Amazed at the spectacle of this group of bloodthirsty, savage children, the officer asks Ralph to explain. Ralph is overwhelmed by the knowledge that he is safe but, thinking about what has happened on the island, he begins to weep. The other boys begin to sob as well. The officer turns his back so that the boys may regain their composure.

CHARACTER LIST

Ralph The novel's protagonist, the twelve-year-old English boy who is elected leader of the group of boys marooned on the island. Ralph attempts to coordinate the boys' efforts to build a miniature civilization on the island until they can be rescued. Ralph represents human beings' civilizing instinct, as opposed to the savage instinct that Jack embodies.

Jack The novel's antagonist, one of the older boys stranded on the island. Jack becomes the leader of the hunters but longs for total power and becomes increasingly wild, barbaric, and cruel as the novel progresses. Jack, adept at manipulating the other boys, represents the instinct of savagery within human beings, as opposed to the civilizing instinct Ralph represents.

Simon A shy, sensitive boy in the group. Simon, in some ways the only naturally "good" character on the island, behaves kindly toward the younger boys and is willing to work for the good of their community. Moreover, because his motivation is rooted in his deep feeling of connectedness to nature, Simon is the only character whose sense of morality does not seem to have been imposed by society. Simon represents a kind of natural goodness, as opposed to the unbridled evil of Jack and the imposed morality of civilization represented by Ralph and Piggy.

Piggy Ralph's "lieutenant." A whiny, intellectual boy, Piggy's inventiveness frequently leads to innovation, such as the makeshift sundial that the boys use to tell time. Piggy represents the scientific, rational side of civilization.

Roger Jack's "lieutenant." A sadistic, cruel older boy who brutalizes the littluns and eventually murders Piggy by rolling a boulder onto him.

Sam and Eric A pair of twins closely allied with Ralph. Sam and Eric are always together, and the other boys often treat them as a single entity, calling them "Samneric." The easily excitable Sam and Eric are part of the group known as the "bigguns." At the end of the novel, they fall victim to Jack's manipulation and coercion.

The Lord of the Flies The name given to the sow's head that Jack's gang impales on a stake and erects in the forest as an offering to the "beast." The Lord of the Flies comes to symbolize the primordial instincts of power and cruelty that take control of Jack's tribe.

CHARACTER LIST

ANALYSIS OF MAJOR CHARACTERS

RALPH

Ralph is the athletic, charismatic protagonist of *Lord of the Flies*. Elected the leader of the boys at the beginning of the novel, Ralph is the primary representative of order, civilization, and productive leadership in the novel. While most of the other boys initially are concerned with playing, having fun, and avoiding work, Ralph sets about building huts and thinking of ways to maximize their chances of being rescued. For this reason, Ralph's power and influence over the other boys are secure at the beginning of the novel. However, as the group gradually succumbs to savage instincts over the course of the novel, Ralph's position declines precipitously while Jack's rises. Eventually, most of the boys except Piggy leave Ralph's group for Jack's, and Ralph is left alone to be hunted by Jack's tribe. Ralph's commitment to civilization and morality is strong, and his main wish is to be rescued and returned to the society of adults. In a sense, this strength gives Ralph a moral victory at the end of the novel, when he casts the Lord of the Flies to the ground and takes up the stake it is impaled on to defend himself against Jack's hunters.

In the earlier parts of the novel, Ralph is unable to understand why the other boys would give in to base instincts of bloodlust and barbarism. The sight of the hunters chanting and dancing is baffling and distasteful to him. As the novel progresses, however, Ralph, like Simon, comes to understand that savagery exists within all the boys. Ralph remains determined not to let this savagery overwhelm him, and only briefly does he consider joining Jack's tribe in order to save himself. When Ralph hunts a boar for the first time, however, he experiences the exhilaration and thrill of bloodlust and violence. When he attends Jack's feast, he is swept away by the frenzy, dances on the edge of the group, and participates in the killing of Simon. This firsthand knowledge of the evil that exists within him, as within all human beings, is tragic for Ralph, and it plunges him into listless despair for a time. But this knowledge also enables him to cast down the Lord of the Flies at the end of the novel. Ralph's story ends semi-tragically: although he is rescued and returned to civilization, when he sees the naval officer, he weeps with the burden of his new knowledge about the human capacity for evil.

JACK

The strong-willed, egomaniacal Jack is the novel's primary representative of the instinct of savagery, violence, and the desire for power—in short, the antithesis of Ralph. From the beginning of the novel, Jack desires power above all other things. He is furious when he loses the election to Ralph and continually pushes the boundaries of his subordinate role in the group. Early on, Jack retains the sense of moral propriety and behavior that society instilled in him—in fact, in school, he was the leader of the choirboys. The first time he encounters a pig, he is unable to kill it. But Jack soon becomes obsessed with hunting and devotes himself to the task, painting his face like a barbarian and giving himself over to bloodlust. The more savage Jack becomes, the more he is able to control the rest of the group. Indeed, apart from Ralph, Simon, and Piggy, the group largely follows Jack in casting off moral restraint and embracing violence and savagery. Jack's love of authority and violence are intimately connected, as both enable him to feel powerful and exalted. By the end of the novel, Jack has learned to use the boys' fear of the beast to control their behavior—a reminder of how religion and superstition can be manipulated as instruments of power.

SIMON

Whereas Ralph and Jack stand at opposite ends of the spectrum between civilization and savagery, Simon stands on an entirely different plane from all the other boys. Simon embodies a kind of innate, spiritual human goodness that is deeply connected with nature and, in its own way, as primal as Jack's evil. The other boys abandon moral behavior as soon as civilization is no longer there to impose it upon them. They are not *innately* moral; rather, the adult world—the threat of punishment for misdeeds—has conditioned them to act morally. To an extent, even the seemingly civilized Ralph and Piggy are products of social conditioning, as we see when they participate in the hunt-dance. In Golding's view, the human impulse toward civilization is not as deeply rooted as the human impulse toward savagery. Unlike all the other boys on the island, Simon acts morally not out of guilt or shame but because he believes in the inherent value of morality. He behaves kindly toward the younger children, and he is the first to real- ize the problem posed by the beast and the Lord of the Flies—that is, that the monster on the island is not a real, physical beast but rather a savagery that lurks within each human being. The sow's head on the stake symbolizes this idea, as we see in Simon's vision of the head speaking to him. Ultimately, this idea of the inherent evil within each human being stands as the moral conclusion and central problem of the novel. Against this idea of evil, Simon represents a contrary idea of essential human goodness. However, his brutal murder at the hands of the other boys indicates the scarcity of that good amid an overwhelming abundance of evil.

CHARACTER ANALYSIS

THEMES, MOTIFS & SYMBOLS

THEMES

Themes are the fundamental and often universal ideas explored in a literary work.

CIVILIZATION VS. SAVAGERY

The central concern of *Lord of the Flies* is the conflict between two competing impulses that exist within all human beings: the instinct to live by rules, act peacefully, follow moral commands, and value the good of the group against the instinct to gratify one's immediate desires, act violently to obtain supremacy over others, and enforce one's will. This conflict might be expressed in a number of ways: civilization vs. savagery, order vs. chaos, reason vs. impulse, law vs. anarchy, or the broader heading of good vs. evil. Throughout the novel, Golding associates the instinct of civilization with good and the instinct of savagery with evil.

The conflict between the two instincts is the driving force of the novel, explored through the dissolution of the young English boys' civilized, moral, disciplined behavior as they accustom themselves to a wild, brutal, barbaric life in the jungle. *Lord of the Flies* is an allegorical novel, which means that Golding conveys many of his main ideas and themes through symbolic characters and objects. He represents the conflict between civilization and savagery in the conflict between the novel's two main characters: Ralph, the protagonist, who represents order and leadership; and Jack, the antagonist, who represents savagery and the desire for power.

As the novel progresses, Golding shows how different people feel the influences of the instincts of civilization and savagery to different degrees. Piggy, for instance, has no savage feelings, while Roger seems barely capable of comprehending the rules of civilization. Generally, however, Golding implies that the instinct of savagery is far more primal and fundamental to the human psyche than the instinct of civilization. Golding sees moral behavior, in many cases, as something that civilization forces upon the individual rather than a natural expression of human individuality. When left to their own devices, Golding implies, people naturally revert to cruelty, savagery, and barbarism. This idea of innate human evil is central to *Lord of the Flies,* and finds expression in several important symbols, most notably the beast and the sow's head on the stake. Among all the characters, only Simon seems to possess anything like a natural, innate goodness.

LOSS OF INNOCENCE

As the boys on the island progress from well-behaved, orderly children longing for rescue to cruel, bloodthirsty hunters who have no desire to return to civilization, they naturally lose the sense of innocence that they possessed at the beginning of the novel. The painted savages in Chapter 12 who have hunted, tortured, and killed animals and human beings are a far cry from the guileless children swimming in the lagoon in Chapter 3. But Golding does not portray this loss of innocence as something that is done to the children; rather, it results naturally from their increasing openness to the innate evil and savagery that has always existed within them. Golding implies that civilization can mitigate but never wipe out the innate evil that exists within all human beings. The forest glade in which Simon sits in Chapter 3 symbolizes this loss of innocence. At first, it is a place of natural beauty and peace, but when Simon returns later in the novel, he discovers the bloody sow's head impaled upon a stake in the middle of the clearing. The bloody offering to the beast has disrupted the paradise that existed before—a powerful symbol of innate human evil disrupting childhood innocence.

MOTIFS

> *Motifs are recurring structures, contrasts, and literary devices that can help to develop and inform the text's major themes.*

BIBLICAL PARALLELS

Many critics have characterized *Lord of the Flies* as a retelling of episodes from the Bible. While that description may be an oversimplification, the novel does echo certain Christian images and themes. Golding does not make any explicit or direct connections to Christian symbolism in *Lord of the Flies*; instead, these biblical parallels function as a kind of subtle motif in the novel, adding thematic resonance to the main ideas of the story. The island itself, particularly Simon's glade in the forest, recalls the Garden of Eden in its status as an originally pristine place that is corrupted by the introduction of evil. Similarly, we may see the Lord of the Flies as a representation of the devil, for it works to promote evil among humankind. Furthermore, many critics have drawn strong parallels between Simon and Jesus. Among the boys, Simon is the one who arrives at the moral truth of the novel, and the other boys kill him sacrificially as a consequence of having discovered this truth. Simon's conversation with the Lord of the Flies also parallels the confrontation between Jesus and the devil during Jesus' forty days in the wilderness, as told in the Christian Gospels.

However, it is important to remember that the parallels between Simon and Christ are not complete, and that there are limits to reading *Lord of the Flies* purely as a Christian allegory. Save for Simon's two uncanny predictions of the future, he lacks the supernatural connection to God that Jesus has in Christian tradition. Although Simon is wise in many ways, his death does not bring salvation to the island; rather, his death plunges the island deeper into savagery and moral guilt. Moreover, Simon dies before he is able to tell the boys the truth he has discovered. Jesus, in contrast, was killed while spreading his moral philosophy. In this way, Simon—and *Lord of the Flies* as a whole—echoes Christian ideas and themes without developing explicit, precise parallels with them. The novel's biblical parallels enhance its moral themes but are not necessarily the primary key to interpreting the story.

SYMBOLS

Symbols are objects, characters, figures, and colors used to represent abstract ideas or concepts.

THE CONCH SHELL

Ralph and Piggy discover the conch shell on the beach at the start of the novel and use it to summon the boys together after the crash separates them. Used in this capacity, the conch shell becomes a powerful symbol of civilization and order in the novel. The shell effectively governs the boys' meetings, for the boy who holds the shell holds the right to speak. In this regard, the shell is more than a symbol—it is an actual vessel of political legitimacy and democratic power. As the island civilization erodes and the boys descend into savagery, the conch shell loses its power and influence among them. Ralph clutches the shell desperately when he talks about his role in murdering Simon. Later, the other boys ignore Ralph and throw stones at him when he attempts to blow the conch in Jack's camp. The boulder that Roger rolls onto Piggy also crushes the conch shell, signifying the demise of the civilized instinct among almost all the boys on the island.

PIGGY'S GLASSES
Piggy is the most intelligent, rational boy in the group, and his glasses represent the power of science and intellectual endeavor in society. This symbolic significance is clear from the start of the novel, when the boys use the lenses from Piggy's glasses to focus the sunlight and start a fire. When Jack's hunters raid Ralph's camp and steal the glasses, the savages effectively take the power to make fire, leaving Ralph's group helpless.

THE SIGNAL FIRE
The signal fire burns on the mountain, and later on the beach, to attract the notice of passing ships that might be able to rescue the boys. As a result, the signal fire becomes a barometer of the boys' connection to civilization. In the early parts of the novel, the fact that the boys maintain the fire is a sign that they want to be rescued and return to society. When the fire burns low or goes out, we realize that the boys have lost sight of their desire to be rescued and have accepted their savage lives on the island. The signal fire thus functions as a kind of measurement of the strength of the civilized instinct remaining on the island. Ironically, at the end of the novel, a fire finally summons a ship to the island, but not the signal fire. Instead, it is the fire of savagery—the forest fire Jack's gang starts as part of his quest to hunt and kill Ralph.

THE BEAST
The imaginary beast that frightens all the boys stands for the primal instinct of savagery that exists within all human beings. The boys are afraid of the beast, but only Simon reaches the realization that they fear the beast because it exists within each of them. As the boys grow more savage, their belief in the beast grows stronger. By the end of the novel, the boys are leaving it sacrifices and treating it as a totemic god. The boys' behavior is what brings the beast into existence, so the more savagely the boys act, the more real the beast seems to become.

THE LORD OF THE FLIES
The Lord of the Flies is the bloody, severed sow's head that Jack impales on a stake in the forest glade as an offering to the beast. This complicated symbol becomes the most important image in the novel when Simon confronts the sow's head in the glade and it seems to

speak to him, telling him that evil lies within every human heart and promising to have some "fun" with him. (This "fun" foreshadows Simon's death in the following chapter.) In this way, the Lord of the Flies becomes both a physical manifestation of the beast, a symbol of the power of evil, and a kind of Satan figure who evokes the beast within each human being. Looking at the novel in the context of biblical parallels, the Lord of the Flies recalls the devil, just as Simon recalls Jesus. In fact, the name "Lord of the Flies" is a literal translation of the name of the biblical name Beelzebub, a powerful demon in hell sometimes thought to be the devil himself.

RALPH, PIGGY, JACK, SIMON, AND ROGER

Lord of the Flies is an allegorical novel, and many of its characters signify important ideas or themes. Ralph represents order, leadership, and civilization. Piggy represents the scientific and intellectual aspects of civilization. Jack represents unbridled savagery and the desire for power. Simon represents natural human goodness. Roger represents brutality and bloodlust at their most extreme. To the extent that the boys' society resembles a political state, the littluns might be seen as the common people, while the older boys represent the ruling classes and political leaders. The relationships that develop between the older boys and the younger ones emphasize the older boys' connection to either the civilized or the savage instinct: civilized boys like Ralph and Simon use their power to protect the younger boys and advance the good of the group; savage boys like Jack and Roger use their power to gratify their own desires, treating the littler boys as objects for their own amusement.

SYMBOLS

Summary & Analysis

Chapter 1

Summary

A fair-haired boy lowers himself down some rocks toward a lagoon on a beach. At the lagoon, he encounters another boy, who is chubby, intellectual, and wears thick glasses. The fair-haired boy introduces himself as Ralph and the chubby one introduces himself as Piggy. Through their conversation, we learn that in the midst of a war, a transport plane carrying a group of English boys was shot down over the ocean. It crashed in thick jungle on a deserted island. Scattered by the wreck, the surviving boys lost each other and cannot find the pilot.

Ralph and Piggy look around the beach, wondering what has become of the other boys from the plane. They discover a large pink and cream-colored conch shell, which Piggy realizes could be used as a kind of makeshift trumpet. He convinces Ralph to blow through the shell to find the other boys. Summoned by the blast of sound from the shell, boys start to straggle onto the beach. The oldest among them are around twelve; the youngest are around six. Among the group is a boys' choir, dressed in black gowns and led by an older boy named Jack. They march to the beach in two parallel lines, and Jack snaps at them to stand at attention. The boys taunt Piggy and mock his appearance and nickname.

The boys decide to elect a leader. The choirboys vote for Jack, but all the other boys vote for Ralph. Ralph wins the vote, although Jack clearly wants the position. To placate Jack, Ralph asks the choir to serve as the hunters for the band of boys and asks Jack to lead them. Mindful of the need to explore their new environment, Ralph chooses Jack and a choir member named Simon to explore the island, ignoring Piggy's whining requests to be picked. The three explorers leave the meeting place and set off across the island.

The prospect of exploring the island exhilarates the boys, who feel a bond forming among them as they play together in the jungle. Eventually, they reach the end of the jungle, where high, sharp rocks jut toward steep mountains. The boys climb up the side of one of the steep hills. From the peak, they can see that they are on an island with no signs of civilization. The view is stunning, and Ralph feels as though they have discovered their own land. As they travel back toward the beach, they find a wild pig caught in a tangle of vines. Jack, the newly appointed hunter, draws his knife and steps in to kill it, but hesitates, unable to bring himself to act. The pig frees itself and runs away, and Jack vows that the next time he will not flinch from the act of killing. The three boys make a long trek through dense jungle and eventually emerge near the group of boys waiting for them on the beach.

ANALYSIS

Lord of the Flies dramatizes the conflict between the civilizing instinct and the barbarizing instinct that exist in all human beings. The artistic choices Golding makes in the novel are designed to emphasize the struggle between the ordering elements of society, which include morality, law, and culture, and the chaotic elements of humanity's savage animal instincts, which include anarchy, bloodlust, the desire for power, amorality, selfishness, and violence. Over the course of the novel, Golding portrays the rise and swift fall of an isolated, makeshift civilization, which is torn to pieces by the savage instincts of those who compose it.

In this first chapter, Golding establishes the parameters within which this civilization functions. To begin with, it is populated solely with boys—the group of young English schoolboys shot down over the tropical island where the novel takes place. The fact that the characters are only boys is significant: the young boys are only half formed, perched between civilization and savagery and thus embodying the novel's central conflict. Throughout the novel, Golding's foundation is the idea that moral and societal constraints are learned rather than innate—that the human tendency to obey rules, behave peacefully, and follow orders is imposed by a system that is not in itself a fundamental part of human nature. Young boys are a fitting illustration of this premise, for they live in a constant state of tension with regard to the rules and regulations they are expected to follow. Left to their own devices, they often behave with instinctive cruelty and violence. In this regard, the civilization established in *Lord of the Flies*—a product of preadolescent boys' social instincts—seems endangered from the beginning.

In Chapter 1, the boys, still unsure of how to behave with no adult presence overseeing them, largely stick to the learned behaviors of civilization and order. They attempt to re-create the structures of society on their deserted island: they elect a leader, establish a division of labor, and set about systematically exploring the island. But even at this early stage, we see the danger that the boys' innate instincts pose to their civilization: the boys cruelly taunt Piggy, and Jack displays a ferocious desire to be elected the group's leader.

Throughout *Lord of the Flies,* Golding makes heavy use of symbols to present the themes and dramatic conflicts of the novel. In this chapter, for instance, Golding introduces the bespectacled Piggy as a representative of the scientific and intellectual aspects of civilization. Piggy thinks critically about the conch shell and determines a productive use for it—summoning the other boys to the beach. The conch shell itself is one of the most important symbols in the novel. The conch shell represents law, order, and political legitimacy, as it summons the boys from their scattered positions on the island and grants its holder the right to speak in front of the group. Later in the novel, Golding sharply contrasts the conch shell with another natural object—the sinister pig's head known as the Lord of the Flies, which comes to symbolize primordial chaos and terror.

CHAPTER 2

SUMMARY

When the explorers return, Ralph sounds the conch shell, summoning the boys to another meeting on the beach. He tells the group that there are no adults on the island and that they need to organize a few things to look after themselves. Jack reminds Ralph of the pig they found trapped in the vines in the jungle, and Ralph agrees that they will need hunters to kill animals for meat. Ralph declares that, at meetings, the conch shell will be used to determine which boy has the right to speak. Whoever holds the conch shell will speak, and the others will listen silently until they receive the shell in their turn. Jack agrees with this idea.

Piggy yells about the fact that no one knows they have crashed on the island and that they could be stuck there for a long time. The prospect of being stranded for a long period is too harrowing for many of the boys, and the entire group becomes silent and scared. One of the younger children, a small boy with a mulberry-colored mark on his face, claims that he saw a snakelike "beastie" or monster the night before. A wave of fear ripples through the group at the idea that a monster might be prowling the island. Though they are frightened, the older boys try to reassure the group that there is no monster. The older boys say that the little boy's vision was only a nightmare.

Thinking about the possibility of rescue, Ralph proposes that the group build a large signal fire on top of the island's central mountain, so that any passing ships might see the fire and know that someone is trapped on the island. Excited by the thought, the boys rush off to the mountain, while Ralph and Piggy lag behind. Piggy continues to whine about the childishness and stupidity of the group.

The boys collect a mound of dead wood and use the lenses from Piggy's glasses to focus the sunlight and set the wood on fire. They manage to get a large fire going, but it quickly dies down. Piggy angrily declares that the boys need to act more proficiently if they want to get off the island, but his words carry little weight. Jack volunteers his group of hunters to be responsible for keeping the signal fire going. In their frenzied, disorganized efforts to rekindle the fire, the boys set a swath of trees ablaze. Enraged at the group's reckless disorganization, Piggy tells them furiously that one of the littlest boys—the same boy who told them about the snake-beast—was playing over by the fire and now is missing. The boys are crestfallen and shocked, and Ralph is struck with shame. They pretend that nothing has happened.

ANALYSIS

The conflict between the instincts of civilization and savagery emerges quickly within the group: the boys, especially Piggy, know that they must act with order and forethought if they are to be rescued, but the longer they remain apart from the society of adults, the more difficult it becomes for them to adhere to the disciplined behavior of civilization. In Chapter 1, the boys seem determined to recreate the society they have lost, but as early as Chapter 2, their instinctive drive to play and gratify their immediate desires undermines their ability to act collectively. As a result, the signal fire nearly fails, and a young boy apparently burns to death when the forest catches fire. The constraints of society still linger around the boys, who are confused and ashamed when they learn the young boy is missing—a sign that a sense of morality still guides their behavior at this point.

Golding's portrayals of the main characters among the group of boys contributes to the allegorical quality of *Lord of the Flies*, as several of the boys stand for larger concepts. Ralph, the protagonist of the novel, stands for civilization, morality, and leadership, while

Jack, the antagonist, stands for the desire for power, selfishness, and amorality. Piggy represents the scientific and intellectual aspects of civilization, as his glasses—a symbol of rationality and intellect—enable the boys to light fires. Already the boys' savage instincts lead them to value strength and charisma above intelligence: although Piggy has a great deal to offer the boys' fledgling civilization, they see him as a whiny weakling and therefore despise him and refuse to listen to him, even when his ideas are good. For instance, when Piggy suggests that the boys find a way to improve their chances of being rescued, they ignore him; only when the stronger and more charismatic Ralph suggests the same thing do they agree to make the signal fire.

Apart from the boys themselves, the signal fire and the "beastie" also carry symbolic significance. The signal fire serves as a barometer for the boys' interest in maintaining ties to civilization: as long as it burns, they retain some hope that they will be rescued and returned to society, but as they become increasingly obsessed with power and killing, they lose interest in the fire. When the fire ultimately burns out, the boys' disconnection from the structures of society is complete. Meanwhile, the beast the young boy claims to have seen also emerges as an important symbol in the novel. At this point, the beast is merely an idea that frightens some of the boys. But as the novel progresses, all the boys tacitly accept the beast's existence. The beast comes to represent the instincts of power, violence, and savagery that lurk within each human being.

CHAPTER 3

SUMMARY
Carrying a stick sharpened into a makeshift spear, Jack trails a pig through the thick jungle, but it evades him. Irritated, he walks back to the beach, where he finds Ralph and Simon at work building huts for the younger boys to live in. Ralph is irritated because the huts keep falling down before they are completed and because, though the huts are vital to the boys' ability to live on the island, none of the other boys besides Simon will help him. As Ralph and Simon work, most of the other boys splash about and play in the lagoon. Ralph gripes that few of the boys are doing any work. He says that all the boys act excited and energized by the plans they make at meetings, but none of them is willing to work to make the plans successful. Ralph points out that Jack's hunters have failed to catch a single pig.

Jack claims that although they have so far failed to bring down a pig, they will soon have more success. Ralph also worries about the smaller children, many of whom have nightmares and are unable to sleep. He tells Jack about his concerns, but Jack, still trying to think of ways to kill a pig, is not interested in Ralph's problems.

Ralph, annoyed that Jack, like all the other boys, is unwilling to work on the huts, implies that Jack and the hunters are using their hunting duties as an excuse to avoid the real work. Jack responds to Ralph's complaints by commenting that the boys want meat. Jack and Ralph continue to bicker and grow increasingly hostile toward each other. Hoping to regain their sense of camaraderie, they go swimming together in the lagoon, but their feelings of mutual dislike remain and fester.

In the meantime, Simon wanders through the jungle alone. He helps some of the younger boys—whom the older boys have started to call "littluns"—reach fruit hanging from a high branch. He walks deeper into the forest and eventually finds a thick jungle glade, a peaceful, beautiful open space full of flowers, birds, and butterflies. Simon looks around to make sure that he is alone, then sits down to take in the scene, marveling at the abundance and beauty of life that surrounds him.

ANALYSIS

The personal conflict between Ralph and Jack mirrors the overarching thematic conflict of the novel. The conflict between the two boys brews as early as the election in Chapter 1 but remains hidden beneath the surface, masked by the camaraderie the boys feel as they work together to build a community. In this chapter, however, the conflict erupts into verbal argument for the first time, making apparent the divisions undermining the boys' community and setting the stage for further, more violent developments. As Ralph and Jack argue, each boy tries to give voice to his basic conception of human purpose: Ralph advocates building huts, while Jack champions hunting. Ralph, who thinks about the overall good of the group, deems hunting frivolous. Jack, drawn to the exhilaration of hunting by his bloodlust and desire for power, has no interest in building huts and no concern for what Ralph thinks. But because Ralph and Jack are merely children, they are unable to state their feelings articulately.

At this point in the novel, the conflict between civilization and savagery is still heavily tilted in favor of civilization. Jack, who has no real interest in the welfare of the group, is forced to justify his desire to hunt rather than build huts by claiming that it is for the good of all the boys. Additionally, though most of the boys are more interested in play than in work, they continue to re-create the basic structures of civilization on the island. They even begin to develop their own language, calling the younger children "littluns" and the twins Sam and Eric "Samneric."

Simon, meanwhile, seems to exist outside the conflict between Ralph and Jack, between civilization and savagery. We see Simon's kind and generous nature through his actions in this chapter. He helps Ralph build the huts when the other boys would rather play, indicating his helpfulness, discipline, and dedication to the common good. Simon helps the littluns reach a high branch of fruit, indicating his kindness and sympathy—a sharp contrast to many of the older boys, who would rather torment the littluns than help them. When Simon sits alone in the jungle glade marveling at the beauty of nature, we see that he feels a basic connection with the natural world. On the whole, Simon seems to have a basic goodness and kindness that comes from within him and is tied to his connection with nature. All the other boys, meanwhile, seem to have inherited their ideas of goodness and morality from the external forces of civilization, so that the longer they are away from human society, the more their moral sense erodes. In this regard, Simon emerges as an important figure to contrast with Ralph and Jack. Where Ralph represents the orderly forces of civilization and Jack the primal, instinctual urges that react against such order, Simon represents a third quality—a kind of goodness that is natural or innate rather than taught by human society. In this way, Simon, who cannot be categorized with the other boys, complicates the symbolic structure of *Lord of the Flies*.

CHAPTER 4

> *Here, invisible yet strong, was the taboo of the old*
> *life. Round the squatting child was the protection of*
> *parents and school and policemen and the law.*
> (See QUOTATIONS, p. 43)

SUMMARY
Life on the island soon develops a daily rhythm. Morning is pleasant, with cool air and sweet smells, and the boys are able to play happily. By afternoon, though, the sun becomes oppressively hot, and some of the boys nap, although they are often troubled by bizarre images

that seem to flicker over the water. Piggy dismisses these images as mirages caused by sunlight striking the water. Evening brings cooler temperatures again, but darkness falls quickly, and nighttime is frightening and difficult.

The littluns, who spend most of their days eating fruit and playing with one another, are particularly troubled by visions and bad dreams. They continue to talk about the "beastie" and fear that a monster hunts in the darkness. The large amount of fruit that they eat causes them to suffer from diarrhea and stomach ailments. Although the littluns' lives are largely separate from those of the older boys, there are a few instances when the older boys torment the littluns. One vicious boy named Roger joins another boy, Maurice, in cruelly stomping on a sand castle the littluns have built. Roger even throws stones at one of the boys, although he does remain careful enough to avoid actually hitting the boy with his stones.

Jack, obsessed with the idea of killing a pig, camouflages his face with clay and charcoal and enters the jungle to hunt, accompanied by several other boys. On the beach, Ralph and Piggy see a ship on the horizon—but they also see that the signal fire has gone out. They hurry to the top of the hill, but it is too late to rekindle the flame, and the ship does not come for them. Ralph is furious with Jack, because it was the hunters' responsibility to see that the fire was maintained.

Jack and the hunters return from the jungle, covered with blood and chanting a bizarre song. They carry a dead pig on a stake between them. Furious at the hunters' irresponsibility, Ralph accosts Jack about the signal fire. The hunters, having actually managed to catch and kill a pig, are so excited and crazed with bloodlust that they barely hear Ralph's complaints. When Piggy shrilly complains about the hunters' immaturity, Jack slaps him hard, breaking one of the lenses of his glasses. Jack taunts Piggy by mimicking his whining voice. Ralph and Jack have a heated conversation. At last, Jack admits his responsibility in the failure of the signal fire but never apologizes to Piggy. Ralph goes to Piggy to use his glasses to light a fire, and at that moment, Jack's friendly feelings toward Ralph change to resentment. The boys roast the pig, and the hunters dance wildly around the fire, singing and reenacting the savagery of the hunt. Ralph declares that he is calling a meeting and stalks down the hill toward the beach alone.

ANALYSIS

At this point in the novel, the group of boys has lived on the island for some time, and their society increasingly resembles a political state. Although the issue of power and control is central to the boys' lives from the moment they elect a leader in the first chapter, the dynamics of the society they form take time to develop. By this chapter, the boys' community mirrors a political society, with the faceless and frightened littluns resembling the masses of common people and the various older boys filling positions of power and importance with regard to these underlings. Some of the older boys, including Ralph and especially Simon, are kind to the littluns; others, including Roger and Jack, are cruel to them. In short, two conceptions of power emerge on the island, corresponding to the novel's philosophical poles—civilization and savagery. Simon, Ralph, and Piggy represent the idea that power should be used for the good of the group and the protection of the littluns—a stance representing the instinct toward civilization, order, and morality. Roger and Jack represent the idea that power should enable those who hold it to gratify their own desires and act on their impulses, treating the littluns as servants or objects for their own amusement—a stance representing the instinct toward savagery.

As the tension between Ralph and Jack increases, we see more obvious signs of a potential struggle for power. Although Jack has been deeply envious of Ralph's power from the moment Ralph was elected, the two do not come into open conflict until this chapter, when Jack's irresponsibility leads to the failure of the signal fire. When the fire—a symbol of the boys' connection to civilization—goes out, the boys' first chance of being rescued is thwarted. Ralph flies into a rage, indicating that he is still governed by desire to achieve the good of the whole group. But Jack, having just killed a pig, is too excited by his success to care very much about the missed chance to escape the island. Indeed, Jack's bloodlust and thirst for power have overwhelmed his interest in civilization. Whereas he previously justified his commitment to hunting by claiming that it was for the good of the group, now he no longer feels the need to justify his behavior at all. Instead, he indicates his new orientation toward savagery by painting his face like a barbarian, leading wild chants among the hunters, and apologizing for his failure to maintain the signal fire only when Ralph seems ready to fight him over it.

The extent to which the strong boys bully the weak mirrors the extent to which the island civilization disintegrates. Since the beginning, the boys have bullied the whiny, intellectual Piggy whenever they needed to feel powerful and important. Now, however, their harassment of Piggy intensifies, and Jack begins to hit him openly.

Indeed, despite his position of power and responsibility in the group, Jack shows no qualms about abusing the other boys physically. Some of the other hunters, especially Roger, seem even crueler and less governed by moral impulses. The civilized Ralph, meanwhile, is unable to understand this impulsive and cruel behavior, for he simply cannot conceive of how physical bullying creates a self-gratifying sense of power. The boys' failure to understand each other's points of view creates a gulf between them—one that widens as resentment and open hostility set in.

Chapter 5

> *"What I mean is . . . maybe it's only us"*
> *(See* QUOTATIONS, *p. 44)*

Summary

As Ralph walks along the beach, he thinks about how much of life is an improvisation and about how a considerable part of one's waking life is spent watching one's feet. Ralph is frustrated with his hair, which is now long, mangy, and always manages to fall in front of his eyes. He decides to call a meeting to attempt to bring the group back into line. Late in the evening, he blows the conch shell, and the boys gather on the beach.

At the meeting place, Ralph grips the conch shell and berates the boys for their failure to uphold the group's rules. They have not done anything required of them: they refuse to work at building shelters, they do not gather drinking water, they neglect the signal fire, and they do not even use the designated toilet area. He restates the importance of the signal fire and attempts to allay the group's growing fear of beasts and monsters. The littluns, in particular, are increasingly plagued by nightmare visions. Ralph says there are no monsters on the island. Jack likewise maintains that there is no beast, saying that everyone gets frightened and it is just a matter of putting up with it. Piggy seconds Ralph's rational claim, but a ripple of fear runs through the group nonetheless.

One of the littluns speaks up and claims that he has actually seen a beast. When the others press him and ask where it could hide during the daytime, he suggests that it might come up from the ocean at night. This previously unthought-of explanation terrifies all the boys, and the meeting plunges into chaos. Suddenly, Jack proclaims that if there is a beast, he and his hunters will hunt it down and kill it.

Jack torments Piggy and runs away, and many of the other boys run after him. Eventually, only Ralph, Piggy, and Simon are left. In the distance, the hunters who have followed Jack dance and chant.

Piggy urges Ralph to blow the conch shell and summon the boys back to the group, but Ralph is afraid that the summons will go ignored and that any vestige of order will then disintegrate. He tells Piggy and Simon that he might relinquish leadership of the group, but his friends reassure him that the boys need his guidance. As the group drifts off to sleep, the sound of a littlun crying echoes along the beach.

ANALYSIS

The boys' fear of the beast becomes an increasingly important aspect of their lives, especially at night, from the moment the first littlun claims to have seen a snake-monster in Chapter 2. In this chapter, the fear of the beast finally explodes, ruining Ralph's attempt to restore order to the island and precipitating the final split between Ralph and Jack. At this point, it remains uncertain whether or not the beast actually exists. In any case, the beast serves as one of the most important symbols in the novel, representing both the terror and the allure of the primordial desires for violence, power, and savagery that lurk within every human soul. In keeping with the overall allegorical nature of *Lord of the Flies,* the beast can be interpreted in a number of different lights. In a religious reading, for instance, the beast recalls the devil; in a Freudian reading, it can represent the id, the instinctual urges and desires of the human unconscious mind. However we interpret the beast, the littlun's idea of the monster rising from the sea terrifies the boys because it represents the beast's emergence from their own unconscious minds. As Simon realizes later in the novel, the beast is not necessarily something that exists outside in the jungle. Rather, it already exists inside each boy's mind and soul, the capacity for savagery and evil that slowly overwhelms them.

As the idea of the beast increasingly fills the boys with dread, Jack and the hunters manipulate the boys' fear of the beast to their own advantage. Jack continues to hint that the beast exists when he knows that it probably does not—a manipulation that leaves the rest of the group fearful and more willing to cede power to Jack and his hunters, more willing to overlook barbarism on Jack's part for the sake of maintaining the "safety" of the group. In this way, the beast indirectly becomes one of Jack's primary sources of power. At the same time, Jack effectively enables the boys themselves to act as the beast—to express the instinct for savagery that civilization has previously held in check. Because that instinct is natural and present within each human being, Golding asserts that we are all capable of becoming the beast.

CHAPTER 6

SUMMARY

In the darkness late that night, Ralph and Simon carry a littlun back to the shelter before going to sleep. As the boys sleep, military airplanes battle fiercely above the island. None of the boys sees the explosions and flashes in the clouds because the twins Sam and Eric, who were supposed to watch the signal fire, have fallen asleep. During the battle, a parachutist drifts down from the sky onto the island, dead. His chute becomes tangled in some rocks and flaps in the wind, while his shape casts fearful shadows on the ground. His head seems to rise and fall as the wind blows.

When Sam and Eric wake up, they tend to the fire to make the flames brighter. In the flickering firelight, they see the twisted form of the dead parachutist and mistake the shadowy image for the figure of the dreaded beast. They rush back to the camp, wake Ralph, and tell him what they have seen. Ralph immediately calls for a meeting, at which the twins reiterate their claim that a monster assaulted them. The boys, electrified and horrified by the twins' claims, organize an expedition to search the island for monsters. They set out, armed with wooden spears, and only Piggy and the littluns remain behind.

Ralph allows Jack to lead the search as the group sets out. The boys soon reach a part of the island that none of them has ever explored before—a thin walkway that leads to a hill dotted with small caves. The boys are afraid to go across the walkway and around the ledge of the hill, so Ralph goes to investigate alone. He finds that, although he was frightened when with the other boys, he quickly regains his confidence when he explores on his own. Soon, Jack joins Ralph in the cave.

The group climbs the hill, and Ralph and Jack feel the old bond between them rekindling. The other boys begin to play games, pushing rocks into the sea, and many of them lose sight of the purpose of their expedition. Ralph angrily reminds them that they are looking for the beast and says that they must return to the other mountain so that they can rebuild the signal fire. The other boys, lost in whimsical plans to build a fort and do other things on the new hill, are displeased by Ralph's commands but grudgingly obey.

ANALYSIS

As fear about the beast grips the boys, the balance between civilization and savagery on the island shifts, and Ralph's control over the group diminishes. At the beginning of the novel, Ralph's hold on the other boys is quite secure: they all understand the need for order and purposive action, even if they do not always want to be bothered with rules. By this point, however, as the conventions of civilization begin to erode among the boys, Ralph's hold on them slips, while Jack becomes a more powerful and menacing figure in the camp. In Chapter 5, Ralph's attempt to reason with the boys is ineffective; by Chapter 6, Jack is able to manipulate Ralph by asking him, in front of the other boys, whether he is frightened. This question forces Ralph to act irrationally simply for the sake of preserving his status among the other boys. This breakdown in the group's desire for morality, order, and civilization is increasingly enabled—or excused—by the presence of the monster, the beast that has frightened the littluns since the beginning of the novel and that is quickly assuming an almost religious significance in the camp.

The air battle and dead parachutist remind us of the larger setting of *Lord of the Flies*: though the boys lead an isolated life on the island, we know that a bloody war is being waged elsewhere in the world—a war that apparently is a terrible holocaust. All Golding tells us is that atom bombs have threatened England in a war against "the reds" and that the boys were evacuated just before the impending destruction of their civilization. The war is also responsible for the boys' crash landing on the island in the first place, because an enemy aircraft gunned down their transport plane. Although the war remains in the background of *Lord of the Flies*, it is nevertheless an important extension of the main themes of the novel. Just as the boys struggle with the conflict between civilization and savagery on the island, the outside world is gripped in a similar conflict. War represents the savage outbursts of civilization, when the desire for violence and power overwhelms the desire for order and peace. Even though the outside world has bestowed upon the boys a sense of morality and order, the danger of savagery remains real even within the context of that seemingly civilized society that has nurtured them.

CHAPTER 7

SUMMARY

The boys stop to eat as they travel toward the mountain. Ralph gazes disconsolately at the choppy ocean and muses on the fact that the boys have become slovenly and undisciplined. As he looks out at the vast expanse of water, he feels that the ocean is like an impenetrable wall blocking any hope the boys have of escaping the island. Simon, however, lifts Ralph's spirits by reassuring him that he will make it home.

That afternoon, the hunters find pig droppings, and Jack suggests they hunt the pig while they continue to search for the beast. The boys agree and quickly track a large boar, which leads them on a wild chase. Ralph, who has never been on a hunt before, quickly gets caught up in the exhilaration of the chase. He excitedly flings his spear at the boar, and though it glances off the animal's snout, Ralph is thrilled with his marksmanship nonetheless. Jack holds up his bloodied arm, which he claims the boar grazed with its tusks.

Although the boar escapes, the boys remain in a frenzy in the aftermath of the hunt. Excited, they reenact the chase among themselves with a boy named Robert playing the boar. They dance, chant, and jab Robert with their spears, eventually losing sight of the fact that they are only playing a game. Beaten and in danger, Robert tries to drag himself away. The group nearly kills Robert before they remember themselves. When Robert suggests that they use a real boar in the game next time, Jack replies that they should use a littlun instead. The boys laugh, delighted and stirred up by Jack's audacity. Ralph tries to remind everyone that they were only playing a game. Simon volunteers to return to the beach to tell Piggy and the littluns that the group will not return until late that night.

Darkness falls, and Ralph proposes that they wait until morning to climb the mountain because it will be difficult to hunt the monster at night. Jack challenges Ralph to join the hunt, and Ralph finally agrees to go simply to regain his position in the eyes of the group. Ralph, Roger, and Jack start to climb the mountain, and then Ralph and Roger wait somewhere near the top while Jack climbs alone to the summit. He returns, breathlessly claiming to have seen the monster. Ralph and Roger climb up to have a look and see a terrifying specter, a large, shadowy form with the shape of a giant ape, making a strange flapping sound in the wind. Horrified, the boys hurry down the mountain to warn the group.

ANALYSIS

The boar hunt and the game the boys play afterward provide stark reminders of the power of the human instinct toward savagery. Before this point in the novel, Ralph has been largely baffled about why the other boys were more concerned with hunting, dancing, bullying, and feasting than with building huts, maintaining the signal fire, and trying to be rescued. But when he joins the boar hunt in this chapter, Ralph is unable to avoid the instinctive excitement of the hunt and gets caught up in the other boys' bloodlust. In this scene, Golding implies that every individual, however strong his or her instinct toward civilization and order, has an undeniable, innate drive toward savagery as well. After the hunt, the boys' reenactment of the chase provides a further reminder of the inextricable connection between the thrill of the hunt and the desire for power. Robert, the boy who stands in for the boar in the reenactment, is nearly killed as the other boys again get caught up in their excitement and lose sight of the limits of the game in their mad desire to kill. Afterward, when Jack suggests killing a littlun in place of a pig, the group laughs. At this point, probably none of them—except possibly Jack and Roger—would go so far as to actually carry out such a plan. Nonetheless, the fact that the boys find the possibility exciting rather than horrifying is rather unsettling.

By this point, the conflict between Ralph and Jack has escalated to a real struggle for power, as Jack's brand of violence and savagery almost completely replaces Ralph's disciplined community in the boys' conception of their lives on the island. Ralph's exhilaration in the hunt and his participation in the ritual that nearly kills Robert is, in a sense, a major victory for Jack, for the experience shakes Ralph's confidence in his own instinct toward morality and order. As befits a power struggle in a savage group, the conflict between Ralph and Jack manifests itself not as a competition to prove who would be the better leader but instead as a competition of sheer strength and courage. Just as Ralph boldly climbed the hill alone to prove his bravery in the previous chapter, Jack goes up the mountain alone now. It is also significant that Ralph discovers nothing, while Jack discovers what he thinks is the beast: while

Ralph does not believe in the beast, the beast constitutes a major part of Jack's picture of life on the island.

Jack increases his leverage within the group by goading Ralph into acting rashly and unwisely, against his tendency toward level-headedness—a manipulation that weakens Ralph's position in the group. Although Ralph realizes that it is foolish to hunt the beast at night, he knows that, in a society that values strength, he cannot risk appearing to be a coward. As a result, he assents to going up the mountainside at night. Ultimately, Ralph's decision to explore the mountain at night costs him the opportunity to prove to the others that Sam and Eric did not see the beast: had the boys climbed the mountain in the daylight as Ralph wished, they would have seen the dead parachutist for what it was. Because they go at night, however, they see the parachutist distorted by shadows and believe it to be the beast. In a sense, the degree to which each boy is prone to see the beast mirrors the degree to which he gives in to his instinct toward savagery. This connection emphasizes the idea that the beast is a symbolic manifestation of the boys' primitive inner instincts.

CHAPTER 8

> "There isn't anyone to help you. Only me. And I'm the Beast.... Fancy thinking the Beast was something you could hunt and kill!"
>
> *(See* QUOTATIONS, *p. 45)*

SUMMARY

The next morning, the news of the monster has the boys in a state of uproar as they gather on the beach. Piggy, who was not on the mountain the night before, is baffled by the other boys' claims to have seen the monster. Jack seizes the conch shell and blows into it clumsily, calling for an assembly. Jack tells the others that there is definitely a beast on the mountain and goes on to claim that Ralph is a coward who should be removed from his leadership role. The other boys, however, refuse to vote Ralph out of power. Enraged, Jack storms away from the group, saying that he is leaving and that anyone who likes is welcome to join him.

Deeply troubled, Ralph does not know what to do. Piggy, meanwhile, is thrilled to see Jack go, and Simon suggests that they all return to the mountain to search for the beast. The other boys are too afraid to act on his suggestion, however. Ralph slips into a depression, but

Piggy cheers him up with an idea: they should build a new signal fire, on the beach rather than on the mountain. Piggy's idea restores Ralph's hope that they will be rescued. The boys set to work and build a new fire, but many of them sneak away into the night to join Jack's group. Piggy tries to convince Ralph that they are better off without the deserters.

Along another stretch of sand, Jack gathers his new tribe and declares himself the chief. In a savage frenzy, the hunters kill a sow, and Roger drives his spear forcefully into the sow's anus. Then the boys leave the sow's head on a sharpened stake in the jungle as an offering to the beast. As they place the head upright in the forest, the black blood drips down the sow's teeth, and the boys run away.

As Piggy and Ralph sit in the old camp discussing the deserters, the hunters from Jack's tribe descend upon them, shrieking and whooping. The hunters steal burning sticks from the fire on the beach. Jack tells Ralph's followers that they are welcome to come to his feast that night and even to join his tribe. The hungry boys are tempted by the idea of pig's meat.

Just before Jack's tribe raids the beach, Simon slips away from the camp and returns to the jungle glade where he previously sat marveling at the beauty of nature. Now, however, he finds the sow's head impaled on the stake in the middle of the clearing. Simon sits alone in the clearing, staring with rapt attention at the impaled pig's head, which is now swarming with flies. The sight mesmerizes him, and it even seems as if the head comes to life. The head speaks to Simon in the voice of the "Lord of the Flies," ominously declaring that Simon will never be able to escape him, for he lies within all human beings. He also promises to have some "fun" with Simon. Terrified and troubled by the apparition, Simon collapses in a faint.

ANALYSIS

The excitement the boys felt when Jack suggests killing a littlun in Chapter 7 comes to grotesque fruition in Chapter 8, during the vicious and bloody hunt following Jack's rise to power and formation of his new tribe. Jack's ascent arises directly from the supposed confirmation of the existence of the beast. Once the boys, having mistaken the dead parachutist for a monster, come to believe fully in the existence of the beast, all the remaining power of civilization and culture on the island diminishes rapidly. In a world where the beast is real, rules and morals become weak and utterly dispensable. The original democracy Ralph leads devolves into a cult-like totalitarianism, with Jack as a tyrant and the beast as both an enemy and a revered god. We see the depth of the boys' growing devotion to the idea of the beast in their impalement of the sow's head on the stake as an offering to the beast. No longer simply a childish nightmare, the beast assumes a primal, religious importance in the boys' lives. Jack uses the beast ingeniously to rule his savage kingdom, and each important character in *Lord of the Flies* struggle to come to terms with the beast. Piggy, who remains steadfastly scientific and rational at this point in the novel, is simply baffled and disgusted. Ralph, who has seen what he thinks is the beast, is listless and depressed, unsure of how to reconcile his civilized ideals with the sight he saw on the mountaintop. But the most complex reaction of all comes from one of the novel's most complex characters—Simon.

Simon's confrontation with the Lord of the Flies—the sow's head impaled on a stake in the forest glade—is arguably the most important scene in the novel, and one that has attracted the most attention from critics. Some critics have interpreted the scene as a retelling of Jesus' confrontation with Satan during his forty days in the wilderness, a story originally told in the Gospels of the New Testament. Indeed, many critics have described Simon as a Christ figure, for he has a mystical connection to the environment, possesses a saintly and selfless disposition, and meets a tragic and sacrificial death. Others tie the scene into a larger Freudian reading of *Lord of the Flies,* claiming that its symbols correspond exactly to the elements of the Freudian unconscious (with Jack as the id, Ralph as the ego, and Piggy as the superego). *Lord of the Flies* may indeed support these and a number of other readings, not necessarily at the exclusion of one another.

Indeed, many differences between Simon and Jesus complicate the comparison between the two and prevent us from seeing Simon as a straightforward Christ figure. Simon, unlike Jesus, is not a supernatural being, and none of the boys could possibly find salvation from the Lord of the Flies through faith in Simon. Rather, Simon's terror and fainting spell indicate the horrific, persuasive power of the instinct for chaos and savagery that the Lord of the Flies represents. Simon has a deep human insight in the glade, for he realizes that it is not a real, physical beast that inspires the hunters' behavior but rather the barbaric instinct that lies deep within each of them. Fearing that this instinct lies embedded within himself as well, Simon seems to hear the Lord of the Flies speaking with him, threatening him with what he fears the most. Unable to stand the sight any longer, Simon collapses into a very human faint.

In all, Simon is a complex figure who does not fit neatly into the matrix framed by Jack at the one end and Ralph at the other. Simon is kindhearted and firmly on the side of order and civilization, but he is also intrigued by the idea of the beast and feels a deep connection with nature and the wilderness on the island. Whereas Jack and Roger connect with the wilderness on a level that plunges them into primal lust and violence, Simon finds it a source of mystical comfort and joy. Simon's closeness with nature and his unwaveringly kind nature throughout the novel make him the only character who does not feel morality as an artificial imposition of society. Instead, we sense that Simon's morality and goodness are a way of life that proceeds directly and easily from nature. *Lord of the Flies* is deeply preoccupied with the problem of fundamental, natural human evil—amid which Simon is the sole figure of fundamental, natural good. In a wholly nonreligious way, Simon complicates the philosophical statement the novel makes about human beings, for he represents a completely separate alternative to the spectrum between civilization and savagery of which Ralph and Jack are a part. In the end, Simon is both natural and good in a world where such a combination seems impossible.

CHAPTER 9

SUMMARY

Simon awakens and finds the air dark and humid with an approaching storm. His nose is bleeding, and he staggers toward the mountain in a daze. He crawls up the hill and, in the failing light, sees the dead pilot with his flapping parachute. Watching the parachute rise and fall with the wind, Simon realizes that the boys have mistaken this harmless object for the deadly beast that has plunged their entire group into chaos. When Simon sees the corpse of the parachutist, he begins to vomit. When he is finished, he untangles the parachute lines, freeing the parachute from the rocks. Anxious to prove to the group that the beast is not real after all, Simon stumbles toward the distant light of the fire at Jack's feast to tell the other boys what he has seen.

Piggy and Ralph go to the feast with the hopes that they will be able to keep some control over events. At the feast, the boys are laughing and eating the roasted pig. Jack sits like a king on a throne, his face painted like a savage, languidly issuing commands, and waited on by boys acting as his servants. After the large meal, Jack extends an invitation to all of Ralph's followers to join his tribe. Most of them accept, despite Ralph's attempts to dissuade them. As it starts to rain, Ralph asks Jack how he plans to weather the storm considering he has not built any shelters. In response, Jack orders his tribe to do its wild hunting dance.

Chanting and dancing in several separate circles along the beach, the boys are caught up in a kind of frenzy. Even Ralph and Piggy, swept away by the excitement, dance on the fringes of the group. The boys again reenact the hunting of the pig and reach a high pitch of frenzied energy as they chant and dance. Suddenly, the boys see a shadowy figure creep out of the forest—it is Simon. In their wild state, however, the boys do not recognize him. Shouting that he is the beast, the boys descend upon Simon and start to tear him apart with their bare hands and teeth. Simon tries desperately to explain what has happened and to remind them of who he is, but he trips and plunges over the rocks onto the beach. The boys fall on him violently and kill him.

The storm explodes over the island. In the whipping rain, the boys run for shelter. Howling wind and waves wash Simon's mangled corpse into the ocean, where it drifts away, surrounded by glowing fish. At the same time, the wind blows the body of the parachutist off the side of the mountain and onto the beach, sending the boys screaming into the darkness.

Analysis

With the brutal, animalistic murder of Simon, the last vestige of civilized order on the island is stripped away, and brutality and chaos take over. By this point, the boys in Jack's camp are all but inhuman savages, and Ralph's few remaining allies suffer dwindling spirits and consider joining Jack. Even Ralph and Piggy themselves get swept up in the ritual dance around Jack's banquet fire. The storm that batters the island after Simon's death pounds home the catastrophe of the murder and physically embodies the chaos and anarchy that have overtaken the island. Significantly, the storm also washes away the bodies of Simon and the parachutist, eradicating proof that the beast does not exist.

Jack makes the beast into a godlike figure, a kind of totem he uses to rule and manipulate the members of his tribe. He attributes to the beast both immortality and the power to change form, making it an enemy to be feared and an idol to be worshiped. The importance of the figure of the beast in the novel cannot be overstated, for it gives Jack's tribe a common enemy (the beast), a common system of belief (their conviction that the mythical beast exists), a reason to obey Jack (protection from the beast), and even a developing system of primitive symbolism and iconography (face paint and the Lord of the Flies).

In a sense, Simon's murder is an almost inevitable outcome of his encounter with the Lord of the Flies in Chapter 8. During the confrontation in the previous chapter, the Lord of the Flies foreshadows Simon's death by promising to have some "fun" with him. Although Simon's vision teaches him that the beast exists inside all human beings, his confrontation with the beast is not complete until he comes face-to-face with the beast that exists within the other boys. Indeed, when the boys kill Simon, they are acting on the savage instinct that the beast represents. Additionally, the manner of Simon's death continues the parallels between Simon and Jesus: both die sacrificial deaths after learning profound truths about human morality. But Simon's death differs from Jesus' in ways that complicate the idea that Simon is simply a Christ figure. Although Jesus and Simon both die sacrificial deaths, Jesus was killed for his beliefs, whereas Simon is killed because of the other boys' delusions. Jesus died after conveying his message to the world, whereas Simon dies before he is able to speak to the boys. In the biblical tradition, Jesus dies to alleviate the burden of mankind's sin; Simon's death, on the other hand, simply intensifies the burden of sin pressing down upon the island. According to the Bible, Jesus' death shows others the way to salvation; Simon's death exemplifies the power of evil within the human soul.

CHAPTER 10

SUMMARY

The next morning, Ralph and Piggy meet on the beach. They are bruised and sore and feel awkward and deeply ashamed of their behavior the previous night. Piggy, who is unable to confront his role in Simon's death, attributes the tragedy to mere accident. But Ralph, clutching the conch desperately and laughing hysterically, insists that they have been participants in a murder. Piggy whiningly denies the charge. The two are now virtually alone; everyone except Sam and Eric and a handful of littluns has joined Jack's tribe, which is now headquartered at the Castle Rock, the mountain on the island.

At the Castle Rock, Jack rules with absolute power. Boys are punished for no apparent reason. Jack ties up and beats a boy named Wilfred and then warns the boys against Ralph and his small group, saying that they are a danger to the tribe. The entire tribe, including Jack, seems to believe that Simon really was the beast, and that the beast is capable of assuming any disguise. Jack states that they must continue to guard against the beast, for it is never truly dead. He says that he and two other hunters, Maurice and Roger, should raid Ralph's camp to obtain more fire and that they will hunt again tomorrow.

The boys at Ralph's camp drift off to sleep, depressed and losing interest in the signal fire. Ralph sleeps fitfully, plagued by nightmares. They are awakened by howling and shrieking and are suddenly attacked by a group of Jack's hunters. The hunters badly beat Ralph and his companions, who do not even know why they were assaulted, for they gladly would have shared the fire with the other boys. But Piggy knows why, for the hunters have stolen his glasses, and with them, the power to make fire.

ANALYSIS
In the period of relative calm following Simon's murder, we see that the power dynamic on the island has shifted completely to Jack's camp. The situation that has been slowly brewing now comes to a full boil: Jack's power over the island is complete, and Ralph is left an outcast, subject to Jack's whims. As civilization and order have eroded among the boys, so has Ralph's power and influence, to the extent that none of the boys protests when Jack declares him an enemy of the tribe. As Jack's power reaches its high point, the figures of the beast and the Lord of the Flies attain prominence. Similarly, as Ralph's power reaches its low point, the influence and importance of other symbols in the novel—such as the conch shell and Piggy's glasses—decline as well. As Ralph and Piggy discuss Simon's murder the following morning, Ralph clutches the conch shell to him for solace, but the once-potent symbol of order and civilization is now useless. Here, Ralph clings to it as a vestige of civilization, but with its symbolic power fading, the conch shell is merely an object. Like the signal fire, it can no longer give Ralph comfort. Piggy's glasses, the other major symbol of civilization,

have fallen into Jack's hands. Jack's new control of the ability to make fire emphasizes his power over the island and the demise of the boys' hopes of being rescued.

We learn a great deal about the different boys' characters through their varying reactions to Simon's death. Piggy, who is used to being right because of his sharp intellect, finds it impossible to accept any guilt for what happened. Instead, he sets his mind to rationalizing his role in the affair. Ralph refuses to accept Piggy's easy rationalization that Simon's death was accidental and insists that the death was a murder. Yet the word *murder,* a term associated with the rational system of law and a civilized moral code, now seems strangely at odds with the collective madness of the killing. The foreignness of the word in the context of the savagery on the island reminds us how far the boys have traveled along the moral spectrum since the time when they were forced to follow the rules of adults.

Jack, for his part, has become an expert in using the boys' fear of the beast to enhance his own power. He claims that Simon really was the beast, implying that the boys have a better grasp of the truth in their frenzied bloodlust than in their calmer moments of reflection. This conclusion is not surprising coming from Jack, who seems almost addicted to that state of bloodlust and frenzy. Jack's ability to convince the other boys that the state of bloodlust is a valid way of interacting with the world erodes their sense of morality even further and enables Jack to manipulate them even more.

CHAPTER 11

SUMMARY

The next morning, Ralph and his few companions try to light the fire in the cold air, but the attempt is hopeless without Piggy's glasses. Piggy, squinting and barely able to see, suggests that Ralph hold a meeting to discuss their options. Ralph blows the conch shell, and the boys who have not gone to join Jack's tribe assemble on the beach. They decide that their only choice is to travel to the Castle Rock to make Jack and his followers see reason.

Ralph decides to take the conch shell to the Castle Rock, hoping that it will remind Jack's followers of his former authority. Once at Jack's camp, however, Ralph's group encounters armed guards. Ralph blows the conch shell, but the guards tell them to leave and throw stones at them, aiming to miss. Suddenly, Jack and a group of hunters emerge from the forest, dragging a dead pig. Jack and Ralph immediately face off. Jack commands Ralph to leave his camp, and Ralph demands that Jack return Piggy's glasses. Jack attacks Ralph, and they fight. Ralph struggles to make Jack understand the importance of the signal fire to any hope the boys might have of ever being rescued, but Jack orders his hunters to capture Sam and Eric and tie them up. This sends Ralph into a fury, and he lunges at Jack.

Ralph and Jack fight for a second time. Piggy cries out shrilly, struggling to make himself heard over the brawl. As Piggy tries to speak, hoping to remind the group of the importance of rules and rescue, Roger shoves a massive rock down the mountainside. Ralph, who hears the rock falling, dives and dodges it. But the boulder strikes Piggy, shatters the conch shell he is holding, and knocks him off the mountainside to his death on the rocks below. Jack throws his spear at Ralph, and the other boys quickly join in. Ralph escapes into the jungle, and Roger and Jack begin to torture Sam and Eric, forcing them to submit to Jack's authority and join his tribe.

ANALYSIS

In the chaos that ensues when Ralph's and Jack's camps come into direct conflict, two important symbols in the novel—the conch shell and the Lord of the Flies—are destroyed. Roger, the character least able to understand the civilizing impulse, crushes the conch shell as he looses the boulder and kills Piggy, the character least able to understand the savage impulse. As we see in the next chapter, Ralph, the boy most closely associated with civilization and order, destroys the Lord of the Flies, the governing totem of the dark impulses within each individual. With Piggy's death and Sam and Eric's forced conversion to Jack's tribe, Ralph is left alone on the island, doomed to defeat by the forces of bloodlust and primal chaos.

Appropriately, Ralph's defeat comes in the form of the hunt, which has been closely associated with the savage instinct throughout *Lord of the Flies*. Ironically, although hunting is necessary to the survival of the group—there is little other food on the island aside from fruit, which has made many of the boys sick—it is also what drives them into deadly barbarism. From the beginning of the novel, the hunters have been the ones who have pioneered the way into the realm of savagery and violence. Furthermore, the conflict between Ralph and Jack has often manifested itself as the conflict between the interests of the hunters and the interests of the rest of the group. In Chapter 3, for instance, the boys argue over whether Jack's followers should be allowed to hunt or forced to build huts with Ralph and Simon. Now that Jack and the forces of savagery have risen to unchallenged prominence on the island, the hunt has thoroughly won out over the more peaceful civilizing instinct. Rather than successfully mitigate the power of the hunt with the rules and structures of civilization, Ralph becomes a victim of the savage forces the hunt represents—he has literally become the prey.

CHAPTER 12

Ralph wept for the end of innocence, the darkness of man's heart, and the fall through the air of a true, wise friend called Piggy.

(*See* QUOTATIONS, *p. 45*)

SUMMARY

Ralph hides in the jungle and thinks miserably about the chaos that has overrun the island. He thinks about the deaths of Simon and Piggy and realizes that all vestiges of civilization have been stripped from the island. He stumbles across the sow's head, the Lord of the Flies, now merely a gleaming white skull—as white as the conch shell, he notes. Angry and disgusted, Ralph knocks the skull to the ground and takes the stake it was impaled on to use as a weapon against Jack.

That night, Ralph sneaks down to the camp at the Castle Rock and finds Sam and Eric guarding the entrance. The twins give him food but refuse to join him. They tell him that Jack plans to send the entire tribe after him the next day. Ralph hides in a thicket and falls asleep. In the morning, he hears Jack talking and torturing one of the twins to find out where Ralph is hiding. Several boys try to break into the thicket by rolling a boulder, but the thicket is too dense. A group of boys tries to fight their way into the thicket, but Ralph fends them off. Then Ralph smells smoke and realizes that Jack has set the jungle on fire in order to smoke him out. Ralph abandons his hiding place and fights his way past Jack and a group of his hunters. Chased by a group of body-painted warrior-boys wielding sharp wooden spears, Ralph plunges frantically through the undergrowth, looking for a place to hide. At last, he ends up on the beach, where he collapses in exhaustion, his pursuers close behind.

Suddenly, Ralph looks up to see a naval officer standing over him. The officer tells the boy that his ship has come to the island after seeing the blazing fire in the jungle. Jack's hunters reach the beach and stop in their tracks upon seeing the officer. The officer matter-of-factly assumes the boys are up to, as he puts it, "fun and games." When he learns what has happened on the island, the officer is reproachful: how could this group of boys, he asks—and English boys at that—have lost all reverence for the rules of civilization in so short a time? For his part, Ralph is overwhelmed by the knowledge that he has been rescued, that he will escape the island after coming so close to a violent death. He begins to sob, as do the other boys. Moved and embarrassed, the naval officer turns his back so that the boys may regain their composure.

ANALYSIS

After Ralph's tense, exciting stand against the hunters, the ending of *Lord of the Flies* is rife with irony. Ralph had thought the signal fire—a symbol of civilization—was the only way to lure rescuers to the island. Ironically, although it is indeed a fire that lures a ship to the island, it is not an ordered, controlled signal fire but rather the haphazard forest fire Jack's hunters set solely for the purpose of killing Ralph. As we have seen, Ralph has worked tirelessly to retain the structure of civilization and maximize the boys' chances of being rescued. Now, when all he can do is struggle to stay alive as long as possible, a deus ex machina (an improbable or unexpected device or character that suddenly appears to resolve a situation) appears, at the last possible moment, in the form of the naval officer who brings the boys back to the world of law, order, and society. Golding's use of irony in the last chapter blurs the boundary between civilization and savagery and implies that the two are more closely connected than the story has illustrated. Ultimately, the boys' appalling savagery brings about the rescue that their coordinated and purposeful efforts were unable to achieve.

Much of the irony at the end of the novel stems from Golding's portrayal of the naval officer. Although the naval officer saves Ralph, the ending of *Lord of the Flies* still is not particularly happy, and the moment in which the officer encounters the boys is not one of untainted joy. The officer says that he is unable to understand how upstanding British lads could have acted with such poor form. Ironically, though, this "civilized" officer is himself part of an adult world in which violence and war go hand in hand with civilization and social order. He reacts to the savage children with disgust, yet this disgust is tinged with hypocrisy. Similarly, the children are so shocked by the officer's presence, and are now psychologically so far removed from his world, that they do not instantly celebrate his arrival. Rather, they stand before him baffled and bewildered. Even Ralph, whose life has literally been saved by the presence of the ship, weeps tears of grief rather than joy. For Ralph, as for the other boys, nothing can ever be as it was before coming to the island of the Lord of the Flies.

IMPORTANT QUOTATIONS EXPLAINED

1.   Roger gathered a handful of stones and began to throw
them. Yet there was a space round Henry, perhaps six
yards in diameter, into which he dare not throw. Here,
invisible yet strong, was the taboo of the old life. Round
the squatting child was the protection of parents and
school and policemen and the law.

This passage from Chapter 4 describes the beginnings of Roger's
cruelty to the littluns, an important early step in the group's decline
into savagery. At this point in the novel, the boys are still building
their civilization, and the civilized instinct still dominates the savage
instinct. The cracks are beginning to show, however, particularly in
the willingness of some of the older boys to use physical force and
violence to give themselves a sense of superiority over the smaller
boys. This quotation shows us the psychological workings behind
the beginnings of that willingness. Roger feels the urge to torment
Henry, the littlun, by pelting him with stones, but the vestiges of
socially imposed standards of behavior are still too strong for him
to give in completely to his savage urges. At this point, Roger still
feels constrained by "parents and school and policemen and the
law"—the figures and institutions that enforce society's moral code.
Before long, Roger and most of the other boys lose their respect for
these forces, and violence, torture, and murder break out as the savage instinct replaces the instinct for civilization among the group.

QUOTATIONS

2.   His mind was crowded with memories; memories of the
      knowledge that had come to them when they closed in on
      the struggling pig, knowledge that they had outwitted a
      living thing, imposed their will upon it, taken away its life
      like a long satisfying drink.

This quotation, also from Chapter 4, explores Jack's mental state in
the aftermath of killing his first pig, another milestone in the boys'
decline into savage behavior. Jack exults in the kill and is unable to
think about anything else because his mind is "crowded with memories" of the hunt. Golding explicitly connects Jack's exhilaration
with the feelings of power and superiority he experienced in killing
the pig. Jack's excitement stems not from pride at having found food
and helped the group but from having "outwitted" another creature
and "imposed" his will upon it. Earlier in the novel, Jack claims that
hunting is important to provide meat for the group; now, it becomes
clear that Jack's obsession with hunting is due to the satisfaction it
provides his primal instincts and has nothing to do with contribut-
ing to the common good.

3.   "What I mean is . . . maybe it's only us."

Simon speaks these words in Chapter 5, during the meeting in which
the boys consider the question of the beast. One littlun has proposed
the terrifying idea that the beast may hide in the ocean during the
day and emerge only at night, and the boys argue about whether the
beast might actually exist. Simon, meanwhile, proposes that perhaps the beast is only the boys themselves. Although the other boys
laugh off Simon's suggestion, Simon's words are central to Golding's
point that innate human evil exists. Simon is the first character in the
novel to see the beast not as an external force but as a component
of human nature. Simon does not yet fully understand his own idea,
but it becomes clearer to him in Chapter 8, when he has a vision in
the glade and confronts the Lord of the Flies.

4. "There isn't anyone to help you. Only me. And I'm the
    Beast. . . . Fancy thinking the Beast was something you
    could hunt and kill! . . . You knew, didn't you? I'm part
    of you? Close, close, close! I'm the reason why it's no go?
    Why things are the way they are?"

The Lord of the Flies speaks these lines to Simon in Chapter 8, during
Simon's vision in the glade. These words confirm Simon's specula-
tion in Chapter 5 that perhaps the beast is only the boys themselves.
This idea of the evil on the island being within the boys is central to
the novel's exploration of innate human savagery. The Lord of the
Flies identifies itself as the beast and acknowledges to Simon that it
exists within all human beings: "You knew, didn't you? I'm part of
you?" The creature's grotesque language and bizarre appropriation
of the boys' slang ("I'm the reason why it's no go") makes the creature appear even more hideous and devilish, for he taunts Simon
with the same colloquial, familiar language the boys use themselves.
Simon, startled by his discovery, tries to convey it to the rest of the
boys, but the evil and savagery within them boils to the surface, as
they mistake him for the beast itself, set upon him, and kill him.

5. Ralph wept for the end of innocence, the darkness of man's
    heart, and the fall through the air of a true, wise friend
    called Piggy.

These lines from the end of Chapter 12 occur near the close of the
novel, after the boys encounter the naval officer, who appears as if
out of nowhere to save them. When Ralph sees the officer, his sud-
den realization that he is safe and will be returned to civilization
plunges him into a reflective despair. The rescue is not a moment of
unequivocal joy, for Ralph realizes that, although he is saved from
death on the island, he will never be the same. He has lost his innocence and learned about the evil that lurks within all human beings.
Here, Golding explicitly connects the sources of Ralph's despair to
two of the main themes of the novel: the end of innocence and the
"darkness of man's heart," the presence of savage instincts lurking
within all human beings, even at the height of civilization.

QUOTATIONS

Key Facts

FULL TITLE
Lord of the Flies

AUTHOR
William Golding

TYPE OF WORK
Novel

GENRE
Allegory; adventure story; castaway fiction; loss-of-innocence fiction

LANGUAGE
English

TIME AND PLACE WRITTEN
Early 1950s; Salisbury, England

DATE OF FIRST PUBLICATION
1954

PUBLISHER
Faber and Faber

NARRATOR
The story is told by an anonymous third-person narrator who conveys the events of the novel without commenting on the action or intruding into the story.

POINT OF VIEW
The narrator speaks in the third person, primarily focusing on Ralph's point of view but following Jack and Simon in certain episodes. The narrator is omniscient and gives us access to the characters' inner thoughts.

TONE
Dark; violent; pessimistic; tragic; unsparing

TENSE
Immediate past

SETTING (TIME)
Near future

SETTING (PLACE)
A deserted tropical island

PROTAGONIST
Ralph

MAJOR CONFLICT
Free from the rules that adult society formerly imposed on them, the boys marooned on the island struggle with the conflicting human instincts that exist within each of them—the instinct to work toward civilization and order and the instinct to descend into savagery, violence, and chaos.

RISING ACTION
The boys assemble on the beach. In the election for leader, Ralph defeats Jack, who is furious when he loses. As the boys explore the island, tension grows between Jack, who is interested only in hunting, and Ralph, who believes most of the boys' efforts should go toward building shelters and maintaining a signal fire. When rumors surface that there is some sort of beast living on the island, the boys grow fearful, and the group begins to divide into two camps supporting Ralph and Jack, respectively. Ultimately, Jack forms a new tribe altogether, fully immersing himself in the savagery of the hunt.

CLIMAX
Simon encounters the Lord of the Flies in the forest glade and realizes that the beast is not a physical entity but rather something that exists within each boy on the island. When Simon tries to approach the other boys and convey this message to them, they fall on him and kill him savagely.

FALLING ACTION
Virtually all the boys on the island abandon Ralph and Piggy and descend further into savagery and chaos. When the other boys kill Piggy and destroy the conch shell, Ralph flees from Jack's tribe and encounters the naval officer on the beach.

THEMES
Civilization vs. savagery; the loss of innocence; innate human evil

KEY FACTS

MOTIFS

Biblical parallels; natural beauty; the bullying of the weak by the strong; the outward trappings of savagery (face paint, spears, totems, chants)

SYMBOLS

The conch shell; Piggy's glasses; the signal fire; the beast; the Lord of the Flies; Ralph, Piggy, Jack, Simon, and Roger

FORESHADOWING

The rolling of the boulders off the Castle Rock in Chapter 6 foreshadows Piggy's death; the Lord of the Flies's promise to have some "fun" with Simon foreshadows Simon's death

KEY FACTS

STUDY QUESTIONS

1. *What does it mean to say that* LORD OF THE FLIES *is an allegorical novel? What are its important symbols?*

Lord of the Flies is an allegorical novel in that it contains characters and objects that directly represent the novel's themes and ideas. Golding's central point in the novel is that a conflict between the impulse toward civilization and the impulse toward savagery rages within each human individual. Each of the main characters in the novel represents a certain idea or aspect of this spectrum between civilization and savagery. Ralph, for instance, embodies the civilizing impulse, as he strives from the start to create order among the boys and to build a stable society on the island. Piggy, meanwhile, represents the scientific and intellectual aspects of civilization. At the other end of the spectrum, Jack embodies the impulse toward savagery and the unchecked desire for power and domination. Even more extreme is Roger, who represents the drive for violence and bloodlust in its purest form. Furthermore, just as various characters embody thematic concepts in the novel, a number of objects do as well. The conch shell, which is used to summon the boys to gatherings and as a emblem of the right to speak at those gatherings, represents order, civilization, and political legitimacy. Piggy's glasses, which are used to make fire, represent the power of science and intellectual endeavor. The sow's head in the jungle, meanwhile, embodies the human impulse toward savagery, violence, and barbarism that exists within each person. Throughout *Lord of the Flies,* Golding uses these characters and objects to represent and emphasize elements of the themes and ideas he explores in the novel.

2. *Compare and contrast Ralph and Simon. Both seem
to be "good" characters. Is there a difference in their
goodness?*

Both Ralph and Simon are motivated toward goodness throughout
the novel. Both boys work to establish and maintain order and har-
mony with the rest of the group and are kind and protective in their
interactions with the littluns. However, as the novel progresses,
we get the sense that Ralph's and Simon's motivations for doing
good stem from different sources. Ralph behaves and acts according to moral guidelines, but this behavior and these guidelines seem
learned rather than innate. Ralph seems to have darker instinctual
urges beneath: like the other boys, he gets swept up by bloodlust
during the hunt and the dance afterward. Simon, on the other hand,
displays a goodness and kindness that do not seem to have been
forced or imposed upon him by civilization. Instead, Simon's goodness seems to be innate or to flow from his connection to nature. He
lives in accordance with the moral regulations of civilization simply
because he is temperamentally suited to them: he is kind, thought-
ful, and helpful by nature. In the end, though Ralph is capable of
leadership, we see that he shares the hidden instinct toward savagery and violence that Jack and his tribe embrace. Although Ralph
does prove an effective leader, it is Simon who recognizes the truth
that stands at the core of the novel—that the beast does not exist in
tangible form on the island but rather exists as an impulse toward
evil within each individual.

STUDY QUESTIONS

3.   *How does Jack use the beast to control the other boys?*

Jack expertly uses the beast to manipulate the other boys by establishing the beast as his tribe's common enemy, common idol, and common system of beliefs all in one. Jack invokes different aspects of the beast depending on which effects he wants to achieve. He uses the boys' fear of the beast to justify his iron-fisted control of the group and the violence he perpetrates. He sets up the beast as a sort of idol in order to fuel the boys' bloodlust and establish a cultlike view toward the hunt. The boys' belief in the monster gives *Lord of the Flies* religious undertones, for the boys' various nightmares about monsters eventually take the form of a single monster that they all believe in and fear. By leaving the sow's head in the forest as an offering to the beast, Jack's tribe solidifies its collective belief in the reality of the nightmare. The skull becomes a kind of religious totem with extraordinary psychological power, driving the boys to abandon their desire for civilization and order and give in to their violent and savage impulses.

STUDY QUESTIONS

How to Write
Literary Analysis

The Literary Essay: A Step-by-Step Guide

When you read for pleasure, your only goal is enjoyment. You might find yourself reading to get caught up in an exciting story, to learn about an interesting time or place, or just to pass time. Maybe you're looking for inspiration, guidance, or a reflection of your own life. There are as many different, valid ways of reading a book as there are books in the world.

When you read a work of literature in an English class, however, you're being asked to read in a special way: you're being asked to perform *literary analysis*. To analyze something means to break it down into smaller parts and then examine how those parts work, both individually and together. Literary analysis involves examining all the parts of a novel, play, short story, or poem—elements such as character, setting, tone, and imagery—and thinking about how the author uses those elements to create certain effects.

A literary essay isn't a book review: you're not being asked whether or not you liked a book or whether you'd recommend it to another reader. A literary essay also isn't like the kind of book report you wrote when you were younger, where your teacher wanted you to summarize the book's action. A high school- or college-level literary essay asks, "How does this piece of literature actually work?" "How does it do what it does?" and, "Why might the author have made the choices he or she did?"

The Seven Steps
No one is born knowing how to analyze literature; it's a skill you learn and a process you can master. As you gain more practice with this kind of thinking and writing, you'll be able to craft a method that works best for you. But until then, here are seven basic steps to writing a well-constructed literary essay:

1. *Ask questions*
2. *Collect evidence*
3. *Construct a thesis*

4. Develop and organize arguments
5. Write the introduction
6. Write the body paragraphs
7. Write the conclusion

<hr>

1. Ask Questions

When you're assigned a literary essay in class, your teacher will often provide you with a list of writing prompts. Lucky you! Now all you have to do is choose one. Do yourself a favor and pick a topic that interests you. You'll have a much better (not to mention easier) time if you start off with something you enjoy thinking about. If you are asked to come up with a topic by yourself, though, you might start to feel a little panicked. Maybe you have too many ideas—or none at all. Don't worry. Take a deep breath and start by asking yourself these questions:

- **What struck you?** Did a particular image, line, or scene linger in your mind for a long time? If it fascinated you, chances are you can draw on it to write a fascinating essay.

- **What confused you?** Maybe you were surprised to see a character act in a certain way, or maybe you didn't understand why the book ended the way it did. Confusing moments in a work of literature are like a loose thread in a sweater: if you pull on it, you can unravel the entire thing. Ask yourself why the author chose to write about that character or scene the way he or she did and you might tap into some important insights about the work as a whole.

- **Did you notice any patterns?** Is there a phrase that the main character uses constantly or an image that repeats throughout the book? If you can figure out how that pattern weaves through the work and what the significance of that pattern is, you've almost got your entire essay mapped out.

- **Did you notice any contradictions or ironies?** Great works of literature are complex; great literary essays recognize and explain those complexities. Maybe the title (*Happy Days*) totally disagrees with the book's subject matter (hungry orphans dying in the woods). Maybe the main character acts one way around his family and a completely different way around his friends and associates. If you can find a way to explain a work's contradictory elements, you've got the seeds of a great essay.

At this point, you don't need to know exactly what you're going to say about your topic; you just need a place to begin your exploration. You can help direct your reading and brainstorming by formulating your topic as a *question,* which you'll then try to answer in your essay. The best questions invite critical debates and discussions, not just a rehashing of the summary. Remember, you're looking for something you can *prove or argue* based on evidence you find in the text. Finally, remember to keep the scope of your question in mind: is this a topic you can adequately address within the word or page limit you've been given? Conversely, is this a topic big enough to fill the required length?

GOOD QUESTIONS

"Are Romeo and Juliet's parents responsible for the deaths of their children?"

"Why do pigs keep showing up in LORD OF THE FLIES*?"*

"Are Dr. Frankenstein and his monster alike? How?"

BAD QUESTIONS

"What happens to Scout in TO KILL A MOCKINGBIRD*?"*

"What do the other characters in JULIUS CAESAR *think about Caesar?"*

"How does Hester Prynne in THE SCARLET LETTER *remind me of my sister?"*

---

2. COLLECT EVIDENCE

Once you know what question you want to answer, it's time to scour the book for things that will help you answer the question. Don't worry if you don't know what you want to say yet—right now you're just collecting ideas and material and letting it all percolate. Keep track of passages, symbols, images, or scenes that deal with your topic. Eventually, you'll start making connections between these examples and your thesis will emerge.

Here's a brief summary of the various parts that compose each and every work of literature. These are the elements that you will analyze in your essay, and which you will offer as evidence to support your arguments. For more on the parts of literary works, see the Glossary of Literary Terms at the end of this section.

ELEMENTS OF STORY   These are the *what*s of the work—what happens, where it happens, and to whom it happens.

- **Plot:** All of the events and actions of the work.
- **Character:** The people who act and are acted upon in a literary work. The main character of a work is known as the *protagonist*.
- **Conflict:** The central tension in the work. In most cases, the protagonist wants something, while opposing forces (antagonists) hinder the protagonist's progress.
- **Setting:** When and where the work takes place. Elements of setting include location, time period, time of day, weather, social atmosphere, and economic conditions.
- **Narrator:** The person telling the story. The narrator may straightforwardly report what happens, convey the subjective opinions and perceptions of one or more characters, or provide commentary and opinion in his or her own voice.
- **Themes:** The main idea or message of the work—usually an abstract idea about people, society, or life in general. A work may have many themes, which may be in tension with one another.

ELEMENTS OF STYLE   These are the *how*s—how the characters speak, how the story is constructed, and how language is used throughout the work.

- **Structure and organization:** How the parts of the work are assembled. Some novels are narrated in a linear, chronological fashion, while others skip around in time. Some plays follow a traditional three- or five-act structure, while others are a series of loosely connected scenes. Some authors deliberately leave gaps in their works, leaving readers to puzzle out the missing information. A work's structure and organization can tell you a lot about the kind of message it wants to convey.
- **Point of view:** The perspective from which a story is told. In *first-person point of view,* the narrator involves him or herself in the story. ("I went to the store"; "We watched in horror as the bird slammed into the window.") A first-person narrator is usually the protagonist of the work, but not always. In *third-person point of view,* the narrator does not participate

LITERARY ANALYSIS

in the story. A third-person narrator may closely follow a specific character, recounting that individual character's thoughts or experiences, or it may be what we call an *omniscient* narrator. Omniscient narrators see and know all: they can witness any event in any time or place and are privy to the inner thoughts and feelings of all characters. Remember that the narrator and the author are not the same thing!

- **Diction:** Word choice. Whether a character uses dry, clinical language or flowery prose with lots of exclamation points can tell you a lot about his or her attitude and personality.

- **Syntax:** Word order and sentence construction. Syntax is a crucial part of establishing an author's narrative voice. Ernest Hemingway, for example, is known for writing in very short, straightforward sentences, while James Joyce characteristically wrote in long, incredibly complicated lines.

- **Tone:** The mood or feeling of the text. Diction and syntax often contribute to the tone of a work. A novel written in short, clipped sentences that use small, simple words might feel brusque, cold, or matter-of-fact.

- **Imagery:** Language that appeals to the senses, representing things that can be seen, smelled, heard, tasted, or touched.

- **Figurative language:** Language that is not meant to be interpreted literally. The most common types of figurative language are *metaphors* and *similes*, which compare two unlike things in order to suggest a similarity between them— for example, "All the world's a stage," or "The moon is like a ball of green cheese." (Metaphors say one thing *is* another thing; similes claim that one thing is *like* another thing.)

---

3. Construct a Thesis

When you've examined all the evidence you've collected and know how you want to answer the question, it's time to write your thesis statement. A *thesis* is a claim about a work of literature that needs to be supported by evidence and arguments. The thesis statement is the heart of the literary essay, and the bulk of your paper will be spent trying to prove this claim. A good thesis will be:

- **Arguable.** "*The Great Gatsby* describes New York society in the 1920s" isn't a thesis—it's a fact.

- **Provable through textual evidence.** *"Hamlet* is a confusing but ultimately very well-written play" is a weak thesis because it offers the writer's personal opinion about the book. Yes, it's arguable, but it's not a claim that can be proved or supported with examples taken from the play itself.

- **Surprising.** "Both George and Lenny change a great deal in *Of Mice and Men*" is a weak thesis because it's obvious. A really strong thesis will argue for a reading of the text that is not immediately apparent.

- **Specific.** "Dr. Frankenstein's monster tells us a lot about the human condition" is *almost* a really great thesis statement, but it's still too vague. What does the writer mean by "a lot"? *How* does the monster tell us so much about the human condition?

GOOD THESIS STATEMENTS

Question: In *Romeo and Juliet*, which is more powerful in shaping the lovers' story: fate or foolishness?

Thesis: "Though Shakespeare defines Romeo and Juliet as 'star-crossed lovers' and images of stars and planets appear throughout the play, a closer examination of that celestial imagery reveals that the stars are merely witnesses to the characters' foolish activities and not the causes themselves."

Question: How does the bell jar function as a symbol in Sylvia Plath's *The Bell Jar*?

Thesis: "A bell jar is a bell-shaped glass that has three basic uses: to hold a specimen for observation, to contain gases, and to maintain a vacuum. The bell jar appears in each of these capacities in *The Bell Jar,* Plath's semi-autobiographical novel, and each appearance marks a different stage in Esther's mental breakdown."

Question: Would Piggy in *The Lord of the Flies* make a good island leader if he were given the chance?

Thesis: "Though the intelligent, rational, and innovative Piggy has the mental characteristics of a good leader, he ultimately lacks the social skills necessary to be an effective one. Golding emphasizes this point by giving Piggy a foil in the charismatic Jack, whose magnetic personality allows him to capture and wield power effectively, if not always wisely."

LITERARY ANALYSIS

---

4. Develop and Organize Arguments

The reasons and examples that support your thesis will form the middle paragraphs of your essay. Since you can't really write your thesis statement until you know how you'll structure your argument, you'll probably end up working on steps 3 and 4 at the same time.

There's no single method of argumentation that will work in every context. One essay prompt might ask you to compare and contrast two characters, while another asks you to trace an image through a given work of literature. These questions require different kinds of answers and therefore different kinds of arguments. Below, we'll discuss three common kinds of essay prompts and some strategies for constructing a solid, well-argued case.

Types of Literary Essays

- **Compare and contrast**

    Compare and contrast the characters of Huck and Jim in The Adventures of Huckleberry Finn.

    Chances are you've written this kind of essay before. In an academic literary context, you'll organize your arguments the same way you would in any other class. You can either go *subject by subject* or *point by point*. In the former, you'll discuss one character first and then the second. In the latter, you'll choose several traits (attitude toward life, social status, images and metaphors associated with the character) and devote a paragraph to each. You may want to use a mix of these two approaches—for example, you may want to spend a paragraph a piece broadly sketching Huck's and Jim's personalities before transitioning into a paragraph or two that describes a few key points of comparison. This can be a highly effective strategy if you want to make a counterintuitive argument—that, despite seeming to be totally different, the two objects being compared are actually similar in a very important way (or vice versa). Remember that your essay should reveal something fresh or unexpected about the text, so think beyond the obvious parallels and differences.

- **Trace**

    Choose an image—for example, birds, knives, or eyes—and trace that image throughout Macbeth.

    Sounds pretty easy, right? All you need to do is read the play, underline every appearance of a knife in *Macbeth*, and then list them in your essay in the order they appear, right? Well, not exactly. Your teacher doesn't want a simple catalog of examples. He or she wants to see you make *connections* between those examples—that's the difference between summarizing and analyzing. In the *Macbeth* example above, think about the different contexts in which knives appear in the play and to what effect. In *Macbeth,* there are real knives and imagined knives; knives that kill and knives that simply threaten. Categorize and classify your examples to give them some order. Finally, always keep the overall effect in mind. After you choose and analyze your examples, you should come to some greater understanding about the work, as well as your chosen image, symbol, or phrase's role in developing the major themes and stylistic strategies of that work.

- **Debate**

    Is the society depicted in 1984 good for its citizens?

    In this kind of essay, you're being asked to debate a moral, ethical, or aesthetic issue regarding the work. You might be asked to judge a character or group of characters (*Is Caesar responsible for his own demise?*) or the work itself (*Is* JANE EYRE *a feminist novel?*). For this kind of essay, there are two important points to keep in mind. First, don't simply base your arguments on your personal feelings and reactions. Every literary essay expects you to read and analyze the work, so search for evidence in the text. What do characters in *1984* have to say about the government of Oceania? What images does Orwell use that might give you a hint about his attitude toward the government? As in any debate, you also need to make sure that you define all the necessary terms before you begin to argue your case. What does it mean to be a "good" society? What makes a novel "feminist"? You should define your terms right up front, in the first paragraph after your introduction.

    Second, remember that strong literary essays make contrary and surprising arguments. Try to think outside the box. In the *1984* example above, it seems like the obvious answer would be no, the totalitarian society depicted in Orwell's novel is *not* good for its citizens. But can you think of any arguments for the opposite side? Even if your final assertion is that the novel depicts a cruel, repressive, and therefore harmful society, acknowledging and responding to the counterargument will strengthen your overall case.

LITERARY ANALYSIS

5. WRITE THE INTRODUCTION

Your introduction sets up the entire essay. It's where you present your topic and articulate the particular issues and questions you'll be addressing. It's also where you, as the writer, introduce yourself to your readers. A persuasive literary essay immediately establishes its writer as a knowledgeable, authoritative figure.

An introduction can vary in length depending on the overall length of the essay, but in a traditional five-paragraph essay it should be no longer than one paragraph. However long it is, your introduction needs to:

- **Provide any necessary context.** Your introduction should situate the reader and let him or her know what to expect. What book are you discussing? Which characters? What topic will you be addressing?

- **Answer the "So what?" question.** Why is this topic important, and why is your particular position on the topic noteworthy? Ideally, your introduction should pique the reader's interest by suggesting how your argument is surprising or otherwise counterintuitive. Literary essays make unexpected connections and reveal less-than-obvious truths.

- **Present your thesis.** This usually happens at or very near the end of your introduction.

- **Indicate the shape of the essay to come.** Your reader should finish reading your introduction with a good sense of the scope of your essay as well as the path you'll take toward proving your thesis. You don't need to spell out every step, but you do need to suggest the organizational pattern you'll be using.

Your introduction should not:

- **Be vague.** Beware of the two killer words in literary analysis: *interesting* and *important*. Of course the work, question, or example is interesting and important—that's why you're writing about it!

- **Open with any grandiose assertions.** Many student readers think that beginning their essays with a flamboyant statement such as, "Since the dawn of time, writers have been fascinated with the topic of free will," makes them sound important and commanding. You know what? It actually sounds pretty amateurish.

- **Wildly praise the work.** Another typical mistake student writers make is extolling the work or author. Your teacher doesn't need to be told that "Shakespeare is perhaps the greatest writer in the English language." You can mention a work's reputation in passing—by referring to *The Adventures of Huckleberry Finn* as "Mark Twain's enduring classic," for example—but don't make a point of bringing it up unless that reputation is key to your argument.

- **Go off-topic.** Keep your introduction streamlined and to the point. Don't feel the need to throw in all kinds of bells and whistles in order to impress your reader—just get to the point as quickly as you can, without skimping on any of the required steps.

---

6. Write the Body Paragraphs

Once you've written your introduction, you'll take the arguments you developed in step 4 and turn them into your body paragraphs. The organization of this middle section of your essay will largely be determined by the argumentative strategy you use, but no matter how you arrange your thoughts, your body paragraphs need to do the following:

- **Begin with a strong topic sentence.** Topic sentences are like signs on a highway: they tell the reader where they are and where they're going. A good topic sentence not only alerts readers to what issue will be discussed in the following paragraph but also gives them a sense of what argument will be made *about* that issue. "Rumor and gossip play an important role in *The Crucible*" isn't a strong topic sentence because it doesn't tell us very much. "The community's constant gossiping creates an environment that allows false accusations to flourish" is a much stronger topic sentence—it not only tells us *what* the paragraph will discuss (gossip) but *how* the paragraph will discuss the topic (by showing how gossip creates a set of conditions that leads to the play's climactic action).

- **Fully and completely develop a single thought.** Don't skip around in your paragraph or try to stuff in too much material. Body paragraphs are like bricks: each individual one needs to be strong and sturdy or the entire structure will collapse. Make sure you have really proven your point before moving on to the next one.

- **Use transitions effectively.** Good literary essay writers know that each paragraph must be clearly and strongly linked to the material around it. Think of each paragraph as a response to the one that precedes it. Use transition words and phrases such as *however, similarly, on the contrary, therefore,* and *furthermore* to indicate what kind of response you're making.

---

7. WRITE THE CONCLUSION

Just as you used the introduction to ground your readers in the topic before providing your thesis, you'll use the conclusion to quickly summarize the specifics learned thus far and then hint at the broader implications of your topic. A good conclusion will:

- **Do more than simply restate the thesis.** If your thesis argued that *The Catcher in the Rye* can be read as a Christian allegory, don't simply end your essay by saying, "And that is why *The Catcher in the Rye* can be read as a Christian allegory." If you've constructed your arguments well, this kind of statement will just be redundant.

- **Synthesize the arguments, not summarize them.** Similarly, don't repeat the details of your body paragraphs in your conclusion. The reader has already read your essay, and chances are it's not so long that they've forgotten all your points by now.

- **Revisit the "So what?" question.** In your introduction, you made a case for why your topic and position are important. You should close your essay with the same sort of gesture. What do your readers know now that they didn't know before? How will that knowledge help them better appreciate or understand the work overall?

- **Move from the specific to the general.** Your essay has most likely treated a very specific element of the work—a single character, a small set of images, or a particular passage. In your conclusion, try to show how this narrow discussion has wider implications for the work overall. If your essay on *To Kill a Mockingbird* focused on the character of Boo Radley, for example, you might want to include a bit in your conclusion about how he fits into the novel's larger message about childhood, innocence, or family life.

- **Stay relevant.** Your conclusion should suggest new directions of thought, but it shouldn't be treated as an opportunity to pad your essay with all the extra, interesting ideas you came up with during your brainstorming sessions but couldn't fit into the essay proper. Don't attempt to stuff in unrelated queries or too many abstract thoughts.

- **Avoid making overblown closing statements.** A conclusion should open up your highly specific, focused discussion, but it should do so without drawing a sweeping lesson about life or human nature. Making such observations may be part of the point of reading, but it's almost always a mistake in essays, where these observations tend to sound overly dramatic or simply silly.

A+ ESSAY CHECKLIST

Congratulations! If you've followed all the steps we've outlined above, you should have a solid literary essay to show for all your efforts. What if you've got your sights set on an A+? To write the kind of superlative essay that will be rewarded with a perfect grade, keep the following rubric in mind. These are the qualities that teachers expect to see in a truly A+ essay. How does yours stack up?

- ✓ Demonstrates a thorough understanding of the book
- ✓ Presents an original, compelling argument
- ✓ Thoughtfully analyzes the text's formal elements
- ✓ Uses appropriate and insightful examples
- ✓ Structures ideas in a logical and progressive order
- ✓ Demonstrates a mastery of sentence construction, transitions, grammar, spelling, and word choice

SUGGESTED ESSAY TOPICS

1. *What, if anything, might the dead parachutist symbolize? Does he symbolize something other than what the beast and the Lord of the Flies symbolize?*

2. *The sow's head and the conch shell each wield a certain kind of power over the boys. In what ways do these objects' powers differ? In what way is* LORD OF THE FLIES *a novel about power? About the power of symbols? About the power of a person to use symbols to control a group?*

3. *What role do the littluns play in the novel? In one respect, they serve as gauges of the older boys' moral positions, for we see whether an older boy is kind or cruel based on how he treats the littluns. But are the littluns important in and of themselves? What might they represent?*

A+ Student Essay

Would Piggy make a good island leader if he were given the chance?

In any group of children, it's a given that some will be popular and powerful while others will be teased and rejected. In the real world, adults use their authority to control these divisions and maintain a balanced group dynamic. In *Lord of the Flies,* however, children must fend for themselves and elect their own leader—and Piggy, wise but scorned, is never seriously considered. Though Piggy is intelligent, rational, and innovative, he lacks the charisma and facility with language that both Ralph and Jack possess, traits that the book suggests play crucial roles in establishing their authority. Piggy may have the tactical smarts to be a good leader, but because he cannot convincingly act the role, he would not be able to marshal the boys if given the chance.

Although his contributions often go unappreciated, Piggy comes up with some of the most important innovations on the island. He sees the conch's potential as a rallying device and firmly believes in its ability to keep operations running smoothly. He understands the importance of taking a census, which the other boys recognize only after the little boy with the mulberry birthmark goes missing and they can't determine how many other littluns were killed in the fire. Piggy's glasses provide the spark for the signal fire, metaphorically demonstrating how intellect can spark great progress. The scholarly, sensible Piggy is a born administrator, one who understands how to categorize and effectively utilize information. He also shows surprising personal strength, both in his ability to tolerate the cruel taunts from the other boys, including his supposed friend Ralph, as well as in his willingness to voice the unpleasant truth about the likelihood of rescue.

However, despite these admirable qualities, Piggy is resoundingly unsuccessful on those few occasions in which he does attempt to lead. He stubbornly holds onto outdated customs, such as the use of the conch, long after Ralph and Jack realize that the shell no longer holds sway over the group. Piggy insists on the rules even when the rules are clearly irrelevant, and this stickler attitude, along with his constant speechmaking and self-righteous complaining, drives people away. Ralph and Jack intuitively know how to rally followers, while Piggy seems to repel them relentlessly. Piggy is so unsuccessful, in fact, that he ultimately dies in the act of trying to lead: He is crushed while waving the conch, fruitlessly ordering others to listen to him.

Piggy's total lack of success in a leadership role suggests that there are significant differences between a "leader" and a "thinker." Ralph has an aura of poise and capability that wins him trust. His authority is rooted in personality rather than innovation—he relies on Piggy for that—and he understands the importance of rhetoric in winning followers. For example, he speaks in the language of rescue, playing into the boys' deepest hopes and fears to bolster his hold over them. Jack wields power effectively as well, and boys are drawn to his glamour and charisma. Jack's leadership is rooted in intimidation, which appeals to the boys once the island turns savage. The boys' negative reaction to Piggy's physical unattractiveness emphasizes the role external personas play in establishing command; the boys' don't so much reject Piggy because he is ugly, but because he does not know how to play the role of a leader.

Piggy's failure as a leader points to an important theme of the novel: the failure of civilization in the face of savagery. Piggy represents rationalism and discipline, the very qualities that Jack himself identifies as making "the English . . . the best at everything." Despite Jack's initial support of rules and regulations, however, *Lord of the Flies* suggests that absent the structures of school, family, and government, which prop up civilization, human beings will always choose anarchy and hedonism over law and order. Piggy represents the wild boys' strongest link to civilization: Once he is killed, the hope of regaining it is lost forever, and only chaos remains.

GLOSSARY OF LITERARY TERMS

ANTAGONIST
The entity that acts to frustrate the goals of the *protagonist*. The antagonist is usually another *character* but may also be a non-human force.

ANTIHERO / ANTIHEROINE
A *protagonist* who is not admirable or who challenges notions of what should be considered admirable.

CHARACTER
A person, animal, or any other thing with a personality that appears in a *narrative*.

CLIMAX
The moment of greatest intensity in a text or the major turning point in the *plot*.

CONFLICT
The central struggle that moves the *plot* forward. The conflict can be the *protagonist*'s struggle against fate, nature, society, or another person.

FIRST-PERSON POINT OF VIEW
A literary style in which the *narrator* tells the story from his or her own *point of view* and refers to himself or herself as "I." The narrator may be an active participant in the story or just an observer.

HERO / HEROINE
The principal *character* in a literary work or *narrative*.

IMAGERY
Language that brings to mind sense-impressions, representing things that can be seen, smelled, heard, tasted, or touched.

MOTIF
A recurring idea, structure, contrast, or device that develops or informs the major *themes* of a work of literature.

NARRATIVE
A story.

NARRATOR

The person (sometimes a *character*) who tells a story; the *voice* assumed by the writer. The narrator and the author of the work of literature are not the same person.

PLOT

The arrangement of the events in a story, including the sequence in which they are told, the relative emphasis they are given, and the causal connections between events.

POINT OF VIEW

The *perspective* that a *narrative* takes toward the events it describes.

PROTAGONIST

The main *character* around whom the story revolves.

SETTING

The location of a *narrative* in time and space. Setting creates mood or atmosphere.

SUBPLOT

A secondary *plot* that is of less importance to the overall story but may serve as a point of contrast or comparison to the main plot.

SYMBOL

An object, *character,* figure, or color that is used to represent an abstract idea or concept. Unlike an *emblem,* a symbol may have different meanings in different contexts.

SYNTAX

The way the words in a piece of writing are put together to form lines, phrases, or clauses; the basic structure of a piece of writing.

THEME

A fundamental and universal idea explored in a literary work.

TONE

The author's attitude toward the subject or *characters* of a story or poem or toward the reader.

VOICE

An author's individual way of using language to reflect his or her own personality and attitudes. An author communicates voice through *tone, diction,* and *syntax.*

A Note on Plagiarism

Plagiarism—presenting someone else's work as your own—rears its ugly head in many forms. Many students know that copying text without citing it is unacceptable. But some don't realize that even if you're not quoting directly, but instead are paraphrasing or summarizing, *it is plagiarism* unless you cite the source. Here are the most common forms of plagiarism:

- Using an author's phrases, sentences, or paragraphs without citing the source
- Paraphrasing an author's ideas without citing the source
- Passing off another student's work as your own

How do you steer clear of plagiarism? You should *always* acknowledge all words and ideas that aren't your own by using quotation marks around verbatim text or citations like footnotes and endnotes to note another writer's ideas. For more information on how to give credit when credit is due, ask your teacher for guidance or visit www.sparknotes.com.

Review & Resources

Quiz

1. Whose responsibility is it to maintain the first signal fire?

   A.   Piggy's
   B.   The hunters'
   C.   Sam and Eric's
   D.   The littluns'

2. What powers does Jack ascribe to the beast after Simon's murder?

   A.   Immortality and the power to change shape
   B.   Telepathy and the power to change shape
   C.   Immortality and telepathy
   D.   Enormous strength and murderous cunning

3. How does the first boy disappear?

   A.   Roger crushes him with a boulder.
   B.   The other boys kill him with their bare hands.
   C.   A boar gores him.
   D.   He burns to death when the signal fire ignites the forest.

4. Who is the first boy to disappear?

   A.   Piggy
   B.   Simon
   C.   Clark
   D.   A littlun

5. Where does the beast go during the day, according to one littlun?

   A.   Into the ocean
   B.   Into the air
   C.   Into the fire
   D.   Into the caves near the Castle Rock

6. Who sees the dead parachutist first?

   A. Ralph
   B. Sam and Eric
   C. Jack
   D. Piggy

7. Which character speaks to the Lord of the Flies?

   A. Phil
   B. Ralph
   C. Piggy
   D. Simon

8. What lures the navy ship to the island?

   A. The fire in the jungle
   B. The roar of the beast
   C. The signal fire
   D. The shortwave radio

9. Whom does Jack strike shortly after his first kill?

   A. Ralph
   B. Francis
   C. Piggy
   D. Roger

10. When Piggy is killed, what else is destroyed?

    A. The shortwave radio
    B. The conch shell
    C. The Lord of the Flies
    D. The signal fire

11. What is Ralph's first act upon being elected leader?

    A. Planning the building of the signal fire
    B. Naming Piggy his chief advisor
    C. Naming Simon the leader of the mystics
    D. Naming Jack the leader of the hunters

REVIEW & RESOURCES

12. What object does Ralph clutch when he talks about Simon's murder?

    A.   The sow's head
    B.   The conch shell
    C.   Piggy's glasses
    D.   A spear

13. Who is the only boy to kill someone on the island by himself?

    A.   Piggy
    B.   Jack
    C.   Roger
    D.   Robert

14. What does Jack suggest the boys use as the "pig" in their dance-like reenactment of the hunt?

    A.   A littlun
    B.   Piggy
    C.   Ralph
    D.   A real pig

15. Which boy treats the littluns with the most kindness?

    A.   Simon
    B.   Jack
    C.   Piggy
    D.   Ralph

16. Which boy would rather hunt than build huts?

    A.   Simon
    B.   Jack
    C.   Piggy
    D.   Ralph

17. Where is Jack's tribe headquarters?

    A.   Next to Ralph's
    B.   On the mountain of the beast
    C.   Deep in the jungle
    D.   At the Castle Rock

18. What tool or tools do the boys use to make fire?

    A.   A flint and steel
    B.   Ralph's tinderbox
    C.   Piggy's glasses
    D.   Matches from the airplane

19. What is the boys' home country?

    A.   England
    B.   Australia
    C.   New Zealand
    D.   Canada

20. Who kills Piggy?

    A.   Ralph
    B.   Roger
    C.   Sam and Eric
    D.   Simon

21. What surrounds Simon's body as it floats into the sea?

    A.   Sharks
    B.   Eels
    C.   A cloud of blood
    D.   Glowing fish

22. Who knocks the Lord of the Flies to the ground?

    A.   Ralph
    B.   Roger
    C.   Simon
    D.   Piggy

23. On what obstruction does the dead parachutist become tangled?

    A.   Tree limbs
    B.   Jagged rocks
    C.   The roof of the hut
    D.   The Castle Rock

24. Who tells Jack where Ralph is hiding in Chapter 12?

    A.   Simon
    B.   Roger
    C.   A littlun
    D.   Sam and Eric

25. Which boy does not dance at Jack's first feast?

    A.   Simon
    B.   Ralph
    C.   Piggy
    D.   Jack

ANSWER KEY

1: B; 2: A; 3: D; 4: D; 5: A; 6: B; 7: D; 8: A; 9: C; 10: B; 11: D; 12: B;
13: C; 14: A; 15: A; 16: B; 17: D; 18: C; 19: A; 20: B; 21: D; 22: A;
23: B; 24: D; 25: A

SUGGESTIONS FOR FURTHER READING

BAKER, JAMES R. *William Golding.* New York: St. Martin's Press, 1965.

BLOOM, HAROLD, ed. LORD OF THE FLIES: *Modern Critical Interpretations.* New York: Chelsea House Publishers, 1998.

GOLDING, WILLIAM. *The Inheritors.* New York: Harvest Books, 1988.

———. *Pincher Martin.* New York: Harvest Books, 2002.

OLSEN, KIRSTIN. *Understanding* LORD OF THE FLIES: *A Student Casebook to Issues, Sources, and Historical Documents.* Westport, CT: Greenwood Publishing Group, 2000.

SWISHER, CLARICE, ed. *Readings on* LORD OF THE FLIES. San Diego, CA: Greenhaven Press, 1997.

WILLIAMS, NIGEL, adaptor. *William Golding's* LORD OF THE FLIES: *Acting Edition.* London: Faber and Faber, 1996.

SparkNotes Literature Guides

Visit sparknotes.com for many more!